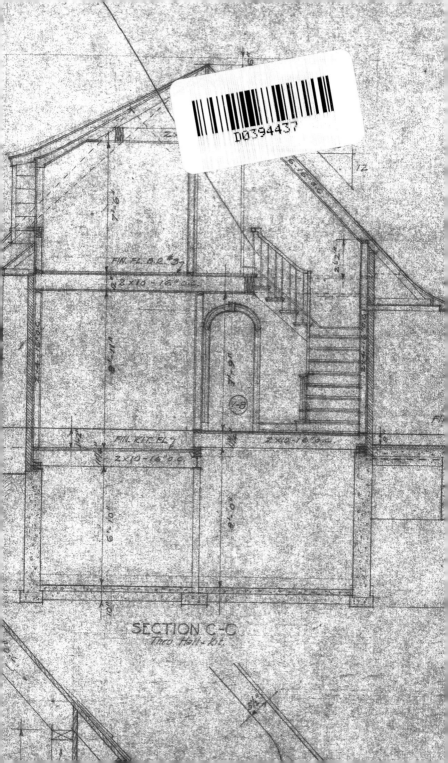

SECTION C-C
Thro Hall · R.L.

RENOVATIONS

John Marchese

RIVERHEAD BOOKS
a member of Penguin Putnam Inc.
New York
2001

RENOVATIONS

A Father and Son
Rebuild a House
and Rediscover
Each Other

Parts of chapters one and fourteen first appeared
in *The New York Times,* in a different form.

Riverhead Books
a member of
Penguin Putnam Inc.
375 Hudson Street
New York, NY 10014

Copyright © 2001 by John Marchese
All rights reserved. This book, or parts thereof, may not
be reproduced in any form without permission.
Published simultaneously in Canada

Library of Congress Cataloging-in-Publication Data

Marchese, John.
Renovations : a father and son rebuild a house and
rediscover each other / John Marchese.
p.   cm.
ISBN 1-57322-174-0
1. Dwellings—Remodeling—Anecdotes.
2. Fathers and sons—Anecdotes.   I. Title.

TH4816.M27   2001   00-062636
690'.837'0922—dc21

Printed in the United States of America
1   3   5   7   9   10   8   6   4   2

This book is printed on acid-free paper. ∞

Book design by Amanda Dewey

*Architectural drawings on endpapers
by Albert E. Milliken
courtesy of Robert Milliken.*

Since the story is dedicated to my father,
I dedicate the book to my mother.

Contents

RENOVATIONS

1.

Tearing Down a Wall

Tearing down a wall is easy. I mean the standard wall in a modern home—half-inch Sheetrock over two-by-four wooden studs. I have ripped down a few now, and I can outline the procedure.

First, I poke a hole in the Sheetrock with a short knife, a serrated eight-inch blade that looks as if it could be on display in a museum of horrible felonies. It looks like a bread knife gone bad. The proper name for it is keyhole saw, and I use my father's. Most of the tools I use are his, except for a sixteen-ounce graphite hammer that friends gave me for my thirty-ninth birthday, just before I left New York City to renovate a house in the country.

After I've cut a small hole with the keyhole saw, I stick my hand inside the wall and feel around for wires to make sure that further cutting doesn't send me flying across the room like an electrified human wrecking ball. If all is clear, I extend the cut through the wall's skin with a regular saw, running as close to a vertical stud as possible. Sheetrock is a sandwich of gypsum and paper. It makes good walls—solid enough to hold family pictures and mirrors—but a person could easily put his fist through it in a fit of rage. Since I've started working on this house I've understood the urge, but never indulged it. With a sharp tool, it cuts easy.

When I've sawed a channel from floor to ceiling, I start pulling on the wallboard, trying to make a sheet open out like a door, prying and working it back and forth until it breaks off. As I do all this tugging and twisting, white gypsum dust pours to the floor and piles in small heaps. It fills my throat and nose. It covers every horizontal and some vertical surfaces. There have been times during the months I've spent renovating when I've padded bleary-eyed and hung-over into the kitchen to find a coat of white dust lining the bottom of my coffee pot. This never bothered me because it seemed to illustrate a large and important truth: Renovating anything is a messy business.

Sometimes the mess is most of the fun. For someone like me, who has spent nearly two decades constructing nothing stronger than sentences, the idea of tearing down a wall and building another is filled with romance and danger. The tools I use—hammers, saws, crowbars, catspaws—seem like an arsenal fit for some swashbuckler. Simply walking around with a tool belt strapped on makes me feel different, more competent and masterful.

One doesn't need to have a great interest in etymology to appreciate the significance of the word "renovate." The definition is full of the promise of new life and vigor, the notion of something better springing out of the dust and dirt. When, for the first time, I picked up the keyhole saw and jabbed it into a wall, I felt that I held in my hand the key to my own renovation. From an inchoate mess of wood and plaster, nails and wire would come a new and better structure, to be inhabited by a new and better man.

After all the Sheetrock is off, I attack the studs. I watched my father do this first, in the damp chill of an unheated second floor as we began to gut my house. He approaches demolition as he approaches much of life, with a dogged, impatient stubbornness, hoping that force and perseverance will make up for subtlety and grace. His idea of tearing out a stud is heavy on the *tearing*, and I've come to believe that he enjoys the demolition process simply because it gives him an excuse to curse.

He whacks, he hammers, he pounds—great thudding blows. *"You bastard,"* he'll yell. *Whack, whack.* The doomed wall lets loose a a shrill scream as a sixteen-penny spike, a nail the size of a pencil, is pulled inch by painful inch from the wood that has been its home for four decades. I have seen him in the midst of a frenzy of destruction, unaware that blood is dripping to the floor from a dime-size patch of skin hanging from his finger.

"You're bleeding," I tell him.

He lifts his hand for a look. "How the hell did I do that?" he wonders. (I have one answer to his question that is not entirely generous, but saying it is another urge I don't in-dulge. He's working for free.) He sticks the filthy finger into his mouth for a moment and then goes back to work.

After we have stripped the second floor to the bare rafters, my father tells me, "Okay, now you're a demolition expert."

I think he is joking.

But when it comes time to start tearing up the first floor on my own, I decide to try flying my pattern. With the Sheetrock I follow my father's procedures, but my approach to the wood is different. I try to coax the old boards out. I want to remove them intact, as if a videotape of the original carpentry were merely running backward and the hammer head were magically sucking the nails out of the boards with each blow. Working this way, it takes me two entire days to remove a few short bathroom walls and a couple of door frames. But the boards could have gone back into another wall—if they hadn't become so warped and twisted over the years as to be unusable.

"Why'd you save this shit?" my father asks when he returns to work and sees that my salvaged wood is worthless. He probably has a theory to answer his question about me, but he doesn't offer it.

This happens nearly a year into my renovation project. Of all the things I'm learning in the process of working on this house, the most complicated, the most frustrating, and the most important thing is finding out about the makeup of the man I call my father.

As I entered midlife, I realized that my father and I shared a name and just about nothing else. No one has ever told me, "Oh, you're just like your father." We had, each of us, built a wall between us, whether we meant to or not. I tried one day to make a list of things we had in common. It was a short list. One thing leapt out at me: Neither of us had ever owned a house.

He had built them, though—scores of houses in his decades working in construction. There were churches, too, and schools and hospitals and power plants. His role in building them was small, and usually invisible to the layman. He was often just one of scores of workers on a site. But I think the lasting presence, the matter-of-fact solidity of everything he has built gives him pride. Most of the things he has had a hand in building will long outlast him.

My father is not a particularly sentimental man, but his relationship with his work, I've come to realize, is strong and complex. A few years ago, when a drive-in theater screen he'd helped put up was torn down, it took him a long time to get over it. Maybe this place was special for him because he'd actually used it—our whole family had watched movies there on summer nights, the gun-metal gray speaker hanging in the window of a car that smelled of cheese curls and Hawaiian Punch. Whatever the reason, after that drive-in was demolished, he spoke about it as if it were a friend who had died.

There were many other places, other walls and ceilings and floors that he'd helped make square and solid. Many of these were places that my father would never feel comfortable returning to—college classrooms and fancy hotels—places he rarely went back inside after the last nail was driven. He was a construction worker; they were built by him but not for him. I remember that he used to drive past them when he was nearby, conducting a slow survey from the curbside, staying on the outside, looking in.

For twenty years, he stayed on the outside of my life in much the same way. When I went off to college, a few weeks before I turned eighteen—the first man in the Marchese family to receive higher education—I stepped tentatively into a new world, leaving behind the world that my father knew. The poet Delmore Schwartz used to love the story of the immigrant father who told his son: "Why should I send you to college? Every course you take makes you more of a stranger." If my father ever felt that, he never spoke up.

We drove to my college in a huge blue Cadillac he borrowed from his brother, the back end so heavy with a trunkload of my stuff that it nearly scraped the roadway all the way to Texas. He walked around the campus for a day looking at the landscaping and the buildings. He never asked me what courses I was taking. It was the last days of a Texas August, and as we shook hands in the horrific heat outside my dormitory, his parting wisdom, I remember, was practical and grounded in his own experience. "That building will stay a little cooler," he told me. "It's plastered." He was in the plastering trade. On that topic, he remained an expert.

A few years later I dropped out of school, filled with the notion of reading what are called the Great Books on my own. I sat with him and my mother over dinner at their favorite restaurant—Friendly's—and told them how I wanted to learn ancient Greek and Latin so that I could read the classics in their original versions. My father stared across the table at me. "What the hell do you want to do that for?" he asked.

It is no wonder that even my haphazard and mediocre education somehow became a wall between us. "You're always reading a book," he said to me a few years ago. "You like that?" He may believe that I'm wasting my time, being dreamy and impractical. Or maybe he suspects he's missing something. Now that he's well into his seventies, what can he do? "I'm as smart as I'll ever be," he said one day. "I guess that's enough."

Of course, when I bought an old house to renovate, what I needed to learn was everything my father already knew. Forget about books. I had too many books. I needed *bookshelves*. Simple carpentry seemed like brain surgery to me. My hands were untrained, their skin as soft as the belly of a puppy. I wanted to learn to hammer and saw and frame and insulate and tear things down and replace them with something better.

I wanted to do what people still call honest work. As we started working—my father and I—the metaphor seemed so appropriate. We would tear down the walls, both literal and figurative. Our time together would turn into the dusty, sweaty, real-life version of one of those beer commercials. *I love you, man.*

I had no idea how hard this would be. It turns out I was equally unarmed with the skills required for the job. For this project, I couldn't go out and buy the tools, and my father had none to lend me.

When the vertical studs have been hammered away, I start to pull out the plates, boards that attach the studs to the floor and ceiling. For this job I use my favorite tool—the

Wonderbar. It is some clever company's improvement on the old crowbar. Like a crowbar, it has nail-pulling teeth on either end, and the same curved shape, like a comma. But with this new tool, the hard steel body is flattened, about the width of a credit card, making it easy to slip under recalcitrant boards and get good leverage for prying. This is the one tool my father actually bought new just for this project.

I wedge the bar between the top plate and a ceiling joist, wiggle it around as if I'm churning butter. When the board refuses to budge, I push the flat side of the bar deeper and then hang on it, hoping my weight will loosen some nails.

"What the hell are you doin'?" my father asks.

My feet are dangling a few inches above the floor. "Trying to get this plate down," I grunt.

"You're usin' the wrong end of the bar."

Oh.

2.

I Should
Have Listened

I told you when you were a kid," my father says. "You should pay attention to what I'm doin'. Someday you're gonna wanna know how to do this."

"Yeah, yeah, yeah," I mutter to myself. I hate it when my father knows he is right. Gloating is an ugly activity when it's done in your direction.

He scolds me like this so often that I can't remember the exact circumstances when he first did so. I think he first said it early in the project, while we were painting the basement, trying to make the place look a little cleaner and brighter. He sidled over to where I crouched, making a big mess with a dripping paintbrush, and took the brush from my hand without asking.

"Here," my father said. "Here's how you set the paint in the brush." He dipped the bristles two inches deep in the gluey white liquid, pulled up his hand until the bristles glistened in the air just above the paint, then tapped the wooden handle against the paint can. Now the paint clung to the brush—no more drips. It seemed like a card trick, obvious and mystifying at the same time.

"That's it?" I said.

"That's it," he said.

Why didn't I know this already? There was more. Why was I met with a disgusted look when I handed my father a hacksaw instead of a wood saw? Why didn't I know the names of all the tools we were using, let alone what to do with them? Why did it take me a moment to run quickly through my internal glossary to check the difference between a joist and a stud when either was mentioned? Why didn't I know all this stuff? I should have paid attention.

In a different way, I guess most children reach an age when they realize they should start paying attention to their parents. Many of us, sons and daughters, wait too long to do anything about it. The neglect makes us sad in retrospect, mad at ourselves for missing an opportunity. "I am angry," the novelist Bobbie Ann Mason wrote not long ago, "that my father died before I could ask him all I wanted to know about the life of a dairy farmer."

With men and their fathers, this tug toward understanding has the strength and predictability of tides. The Man Movement guru Robert Bly noticed the need among the guys with whom he hiked into the woods to bang on drums. "Somewhere around forty," Bly wrote, "a movement toward the father takes place naturally—a desire to see him more clearly and to draw closer to him. This happens unexplainably, almost as if on a biological timetable."

So there I was, standing on the station platform of middle age, like a dutiful accountant on his daily commute, train-spotting my biological timetable. For the first time in years, I was trying to listen to my father, to pay attention. And there was a faint theme becoming audible, like a soft phrase whispered by the woodwinds in the first movement of a sprawling symphony.

For instance: We stand behind the house trying to decide the best way to dress up the foundation. A lot of house renovation involves standing in a group and staring at something for a long time. The concrete walls that hold up my house are fully exposed in the back, rising about eight feet out of the rocky ground. There is a series of bumpy horizontal lines running across the concrete where successive layers were poured atop each other. The concrete has aged to a dun color. We stare and stare.

"I'd like to cover that with cedar shakes," I say.

"Nah," he says back.

We return to silent staring.

"Why not?" I ask at last.

"How ya gonna nail them on cement? You'd have to put up furring strips. You're gonna need some kind of trim strip at the top where it meets the siding. It'd be a pain-in-the-ass job."

"So what's wrong with that?"

My father shifts his gaze from the wall and looks over at me. "You're dreamin'," he says. "You're dreamin' again."

For a long time, with a certain grudging affection, I have referred to my father—even to his face—as Mister Worst Case Scenario. He does have his enthusiasms. I have heard him talk many times about a Reuben sandwich as if it were a cherished aria in his favorite opera. He enjoys building things and making vegetables grow. My father's laugh, when it comes, is genuine, a quick, loud bark. But it doesn't come that often, and mostly he seems to live life assuming that some awful cosmic catastrophe will darken the very stars above him and he will wake to find the sun has burned out. He is the kind of man, I'm convinced, who would purchase insurance for his insurance.

I'm not sure how he got that way, but I'd like to find out, because I often seem to be afflicted by the same negative outlook. When I am honest with myself, I worry that my father's somber tones have the power to color everything I see, to alter all my choices and hopes. My father may think I'm a dreamer, but what dreams I have are not nearly as bright as I would like.

For years, there was just one picture I kept of my father. It was taken at a party in the seventies, while I was away at college, and mailed to me by the shutterbug, my mother. She has an idiosyncratic way of framing a photograph. I have a whole box of snapshots she has sent over the years which I could label "foreheads and limbs of relatives." This particular photo of my father cuts off his bulging belly but leaves his upper body intact. He is wearing a pith helmet that he picked up while in the navy in the South Pacific. The camera lens has caught his round face at a slight angle, and, though he rarely drinks, he looks both bemused and a little tipsy. On the back of the picture my mother has written "The Hunter." But there is such a soft compliance in my father's tentative grin, so little aggression, that he seems more like prey.

When I was a kid in the sixties and the economy was booming, construction was everywhere, and my father was a loud, dirty, metal-lunch-bucket kind of guy—a hardhat. He was in his forties and fleshy; he looked a little like Jackie Gleason. And, like Gleason's character Ralph Kramden, he was a screamer.

If a sociologist had studied my father, he would probably have been classified as a member of what came to be called The Silent Majority. But not at home. We lived in the first-floor apartment of a thin little two-story house separated from our neighbors only by a driveway. My mother would try to shush him as he yelled and ranted and went off on loud disquisitions about politics. My father's political philosophy didn't stray much beyond the policies of his labor union— the AFL–CIO—which still had lots of muscle then. Hubert Humphrey was a god to my father, a champion of the blue-collar working stiff, a populist who had earned the title.

It must have seemed then that America's prosperity would last forever, and that our family's fortunes would keep climbing, too. Things were going so well that my father was able to buy a brand-new gold Pontiac Catalina in 1966. We used it the next summer to take the only family vacation I can remember—a trek to the World's Fair in Montreal. My father taught me to swim that summer by throwing me into the deep end of a powder-blue, chlorine-saturated pool at Floyd's, a roadside motel somewhere near the Thousand

Islands. While I flailed around he laughed like crazy and told my mother to mind her own business. "See," I remember him telling me, "you can swim."

My father's sense of himself, I think, was built on a foundation of simple but well-paid work and a feeling that he could place his family firmly in the middle class, if only its lower echelons. I doubt he could sense it coming, but the foundation he stood on in the fifties and sixties would nearly collapse in the seventies. Eventually, his confidence seemed to weaken with it.

Some of it was a long-term process. His trade was lathing: he put up the wire mesh on which plasterers stuck their "mud." Plasterers were perhaps the last link to the artisans of the past, and even if they worked fast, their scooping and smoothing was an antiquated art. Their hocks and trowels might as well have been museum pieces. With lath and plaster, four stages were required to finish a wall, with time out to let the mud dry. A couple workers with a load of Sheetrock and a screw gun could do the same job in a day. In effect, my father was becoming obsolete.

Meanwhile, the entire construction industry was headed for an extended slump, dealt double blows in the seventies by speeding inflation and the oil crisis. My father had always gone through periods of being unemployed, but in the years leading up to my leaving home, there seemed to be longer and more frequent stretches when he was out of work. After I left for college, he finally accepted defeat and took a low-paying but secure job with the city government, shuffling paperwork for government-financed construction projects. Having come down off the scaffold, he lost his footing. I wasn't paying much attention to him in those years, but it seemed that gradually, trapped in listless rooms with time-serving government workers, he became more and more list-less himself. My father grew quiet.

So now that he's scolding me for not listening to him, all I can think is, *What* should *I have listened to?* He wasn't a man with a knack for aphorism. He never put his arm around my shoulders as we walked on a country road and with frank humor told me how things worked with girls. His speeches on the virtues of the working man always struck me as party-line bluster, and some of our worst arguments were about the benefits of labor unions. As someone who'd never worked, I heard the call to labor solidarity as the siren song of medioc-rity. Hubert Humphrey struck me as a political hack who'd sold his soul to special interests of organized labor, big-bellied cigar chompers.

"Anything you got," my father would yell, "you got because of unions."

Big deal, I'd think. *What do we have?*

What I never considered then was that my father was just a normal, average guy, someone caught in the grip of duty, someone who got satisfaction from being a provider, even if it meant the extinction of his own dreams. My childhood seems so dated that when I try to remember it, the images I'm able to conjure are black and white, flickering on the screen of a little TV set dressed with rabbit ears. Sure, our family was more like the Kramdens than the Cleavers, but ours was a successful blue-collar home. My mother never had to work. My father *only* worked. I couldn't have imagined him putting down his lunch bucket one night and sitting us down to say, "I'm sick of this responsibility. I need some time for me." We would have laughed at him.

What was there to listen to? In the background, way down low, there was a steady rumble, one that I'm only beginning to understand. He went to work every morning, and he came home every night. *Every* night. He didn't stop off somewhere for a couple. He was there, ready to eat, ready to assume his place as the head of the family. If he went out at night it was most likely to help one of his work buddies remodel his own house. This was my father's way of saying *This is what men do*. It was a message delivered daily in code, and it was up to me to learn to decipher it. Eighteen years went by with that nearly silent song playing. Then I left home and became more and more a stranger. My father was still sending messages, but I had stopped listening.

Now I'm nearly forty years old, and I don't know a god-damn thing. And I'm going to jump in the deep end—buy an old house and try to fix it up myself, with my father helping. When it came time to get to work, maybe I would learn to pay attention at last. At least I had good reason to try.

3.

Where I Lived
(If You Call It Living)
What I Lived For

By the time I was thirty-eight years old, I had lived in seventeen places. The last sixteen all came after that sweltering day my father left me in front of my college dormitory in Texas. The most recent was an illegal one-bedroom sublet in the East Village of Manhattan, where I couldn't put my name on the mailbox and where I snuck around to avoid the superintendent, who for the entire first year of my residence glared at me each time we met in the hall or elevator and asked in a strong Albanian accent, "Who *arrre* you?" The apartment was cheap and decent, and the neighborhood wasn't bad. The noise started at seven in the morning, when teachers in the schoolyard behind my kitchen began shouting into megaphones. There was a brief break in the din twenty-two hours later, when loud Italian-American men finally stopped smacking metal trash cans on the sidewalk. In a stroll around the block, I could buy cat food, milk, sex with a stranger, Ukrainian delicacies, and probably any drug I wanted.

Two things brought me to New York in the first place: a woman and my career. It seemed that just about everybody else I had met during my years in the city had moved there for the sake of his or her career. I had spent most of my twenties not very successfully trying to make a living as a musician. By the time I was thirty, I'd somehow become a journalist, writing about business and politics and restaurants for a good regional magazine. It could have been a nice, comfortable life, but I felt an urge to go national. From what I could tell, going national in my business required moving to the equivalent of a little medieval village that existed in a few square blocks of Manhattan. Once there, you'd wave your arms and jump up and down and hope to grab the attention of the dozen or so burghers who run the place. I landed in Brooklyn in 1989, one of the teeming masses of literate immigrants from the provinces who make Park Slope or Cobble Hill (or, in my case, Carroll Gardens) their own Ellis Island. Even then, I promised myself that as soon as I had made my contacts, I'd get the hell out. Within a few years I'd made plenty of contacts, but I kept hanging around for one more good assignment, one more lunch, one more cocktail party, one more free movie preview. I might never get accustomed to the guys smashing trash cans in the urban predawn, but there was a background noise in the other part of life that had created a familiar and comfortable environment for me. Mostly, it was the sound of people talking about their careers.

My life could often be quite social, and someone like my father would look at what I did for a living and scoff at the notion that it resembled anything like a job. But more and more, I realized that *everything* I did was work, whether research in the library or having a beer with an editor friend. And as the years passed and the assignments added up, much of that work seemed increasingly ridiculous to me. It was probably my own fault, for I was averse to specialization. I took assignments to write about everything from boxer shorts to aging rock stars. Nothing added up. I felt I was doing a sideshow act off the midway at the vanity fair. That's a dangerous feeling in Manhattan, where you are what you do.

Just before moving to New York, I had spent a summer living in a rented house in the country. This was the early days of laptop computers, and at the time an ubiquitous ad ran in newspapers and magazines showing a man (a writer, according to the copy, with his first big national magazine assignment) sitting on his deck in the mountains, a cup of coffee and a portable computer on his rough-hewn table, and nothing except lush green forest to distract him. That summer was the closest I'd ever come to living a life that advertisers would envision (except for certain antacid commercials). Since then, my goal had been trying to figure out how to get back into the hills. That was the life I wanted.

Sometimes, I had fantasies of the far-off places I would move to (Montana for a while, Washington state for a time) and even made a few scouting trips. There is a season in our lives, Thoreau wrote, when we begin to consider every spot as the possible location for a house. But that turned out not to be true for me. Ultimately, I was always drawn back to the homely honeymoon resort area near where I grew up, the Poconos. For some reason, those tight, rounded hills seemed to open to embrace me. Now that I was finally ready to sink some roots, no other place seemed like somewhere I could ever comfortably call home.

I was also entering another peculiar time in my life. I had either missed the normal benchmarks of adulthood—college graduation, steady job, marriage, home ownership—or was so late in reaching them that it caught me by surprise when my midlife crisis came early.

Sometime in my second year living alone in Manhattan, I began to encounter, with troubling frequency, strangers sobbing in public. Initially, I thought it was simply chance that led me to these sad people. It started one afternoon when I was walking west just a block from my apartment and a woman coming in the opposite direction caught my eye. I had learned not to make much eye contact on this block because streetwalkers plied their trade there. Over some months, I had begun to nod politely at a few of the women. That stopped one evening when a new girl took my politeness to mean she should give me a painful, squeezing solicitation by the fire hydrant outside Dr. Schwartz's office. Since then, I'd been circumspect. But I could tell this woman wasn't a hooker.

She was well dressed and moved as if she were on her way to a business meeting, but she slouched as if she were carrying a heavy sack over her shoulder. Tears eroded her makeup. When I gazed at her a moment too long, she met me with a look that requested no help or pity. She gave me a hard stare that said, *Yeah, I'm crying. This is how life is.*

A few days later, in the same neighborhood, a lowing sound of sadness came from an open window as I passed—a woman's legato, plaintive moan—and within a month, I saw a woman standing tearfully in a subway station, waiting for the train. Not long after that, I strode to a blocked intersection in Chelsea and waited behind a young man leaning against a lamppost on Sixth Avenue, his head stuck into the crook of his elbow, tears dripping to the pavement from moist tracks on his cheeks.

It seemed strange at first to be let into this world of pain. I had read Yeats's line—"For the world's more full of weeping than you can understand"—and within a few short months, without even trying, had gathered half a dozen cases of grief. But, as the poet said, I hadn't come close to comprehending them. I would report to friends over cocktails, "I saw another person crying today on the street." Had I been chosen to become a witness to this common gloom? By that time, I'd been around New York for five years and had lived in another big city for more than a decade. There were millions of stories in both towns, and the chances were that lots of them ended sadly. Still, I had never noticed anyone crying in public until now.

Then it struck me that I had been let into this because I had become a fellow traveler in sorrow. While I had no clue what these people were crying about, there were many days when I felt a powerful urge to stop and join them. This feeling had a lot to do with the point I had reached in life—not exactly Dante's "path diverging in the dark wood," but more a litter-strewn corner under a lonely lamppost at the intersection of Sixth Avenue and somewhere. Mine was a modern sorrow. It had a lot to do with where I lived and what I lived for.

There's a John Cheever story that I've read again and again called "A Vision of the World," and in it is a scene in which the narrator, Cheever's characteristic dreamy suburban husband, comes home to find his wife sobbing. When he asks her what's wrong, she tells him that she knows her life is pretty wonderful, but she feels that at any moment she could be switched off, like a character in an old black-and-white television situation comedy.

"My wife is often sad," the narrator tells us, "because her sadness is not a sad sadness, sorry because her sorrow is not a crushing sorrow. She grieves because her grief is not an acute grief, and when I tell her that this sorrow over the inadequacies of her sorrow may be a new hue in the spectrum of human pain, she is not consoled."

Something in this description stuck with me, captured some aspect of what I was feeling. I knew that I certainly was not painting a new hue in the spectrum of human pain, but I nevertheless felt miserable because my misery seemed so arbitrary and needless. I also was living a life that in many ways seemed like a television situation comedy, even if mine was in color. My friends and I led complicated, neurotic, even glamorous lives. Many of the people I knew identified, justifiably, with the characters of *Seinfeld* or *Mad About You* and all their lesser imitators.

For us, irony was everything.

While I was living in a converted factory loft in Brooklyn with the woman who had lured me to New York, we would sometimes sit finishing our wine after dinner and stare out the huge windows at the glowing buildings of Manhattan.

"Would you be sad if I died?" she'd ask.

"For a while," I'd say, with a tone of mock sophistication. "But life would go on."

And our life together went on fairly well. Until, that is, I decided I really wanted a house in the country. It became a nearly continuous daydream. From my desk in our apartment, I would stare through the big windows at the spire of the Empire State Building—all the time thinking of the country life. Meanwhile, my girlfriend seemed to regard my rural fantasies with increasing boredom, finally ignoring them altogether. She was desperately trying to make it in the city. She agonized constantly over her relative position on the masthead of a major national magazine, over which of her rivals were more in favor than she. It seemed that her fondest dream was to be picked by her boss to lunch conspicuously at the Four Seasons. And there I was, talking all the time about running away to the woods.

"Why won't you buy into my dream?" I would shout at her, with mock anger. A haze of irony clouded even our most important arguments. It eventually broke us up. And no matter what we did, we couldn't get back together. *Click.* How easily I could be turned off.

Next, after years of scraping and working mostly for fledgling or second-class publications, I was going to be offered a job at a very prestigious place. The editor I worked with assured me it was a done deal. But somehow the job went to someone else. *Click.*

Soon, my stories for magazines were becoming more and more difficult to get through the editing process. I reached the point where I would take assignments and lose interest halfway into the reporting. *Click.* To heap on the detail here would needlessly punish both writer and reader. I was spinning down in a quite typical spiral, finally hitting a low point where I started to spend days in bed after largely sleepless, boozy nights, letting the phone ring unanswered, rising at dark for breakfast. I was cracking up.

I hunted down a famous essay on cracking up by F. Scott Fitzgerald. To my amazement, there was an uncanny similarity between his thoughts and Cheever's. Fitzgerald, of course, had known great success and had always been on a boozy slide. But when a middle-age melancholy crept over him, Fitzgerald packed a bag and, he wrote, "went off a thousand miles to think it over. . . . I only wanted absolute quiet to think out why I had developed such a sad attitude toward sadness, a melancholy attitude toward melancholy and a tragic attitude toward tragedy . . ."

I didn't need to go a thousand miles. A hundred or so seemed enough. But I needed quiet and I needed to be out of the city, somewhere in those hills that roll out into my hometown. If I was foundering, I felt I could be buoyed by the sheer busy-ness of work—work I'd never done before, work that seemed somehow more real than any I'd done before. I knew my father would help me because he'd promised to do it once before, when I was in much better shape. In the mud-luscious days of late winter I began my search—for a house and for whatever else I would find with it.

I picked up the Cheever story yet again. The narrator considers leaving his wife, who's sad because of the inadequacies of her sorrows. He could make it on his own, he thinks, but "I could not bring myself to leave my lawns and gardens, I could not part with the porch screens that I have repaired and painted, I cannot divorce myself from the serpentine brick walk I have laid ... and so, while my chains are forged of turf and house paint, they will still bind me until I die."

At this moment in my life, I didn't envy Cheever just for his graceful writing. *Chains forged of turf and house paint!* I decided to take him literally.

This was a prescription.

4.

Home Again

And so I was going back home again, to pick up my father and search for a new home for myself. When I was growing up in Scranton, it was a place, as Alfred Kazin wrote of his neighborhood in Brooklyn, "that measured all success by our skill at getting away from it." I had gotten away for a long time. Was it some kind of defeat to come back? I hoped not.

Scranton is a small city, tidy and shabby simultaneously, with a nugget of attractive buildings in the center of town and then a skewed grid of streets lined mostly with slanting wood-frame homes, singles and duplexes, that climb the hills out of the valley of the Lackawanna River. Our house was on the north side of town and sat at the base of a small hill whose top was once the entrance to a coal mine. As kids we played around the old mine, and we knew that in this town the ground could drop from underneath you at any minute if the weak support of a hidden mine shaft gave way. Later, as teenagers drinking beer on the railroad tracks by the river, we always assumed that if you stuck your foot into the water your toes might not come back out. And that seemed perfectly normal. That was Scranton, a city whose brief spell of prosperity was mortgaged against the future, where some folks got rich and then ran, leaving the place dangerously pockmarked and polluted.

My father grew up in this city when it was a boomtown, in the shadow of the Marvine breaker, named after one of the coal companies that ran the town, gave it a reason to exist, and dominated the economy from the turn of the century into the Depression. Scranton was the center of the country's anthracite coal region. That meant there was work of the dangerous, wet, dirty, backbreaking kind that attracted immigrants like my grandfather Valentino Marchese, a former Alpine tunnel digger who arrived in the town before the First World War and began his family in 1923: Giovanni, my father, who never used the Italian version of his name; Felicia, who would always call herself Phyllis; Santino, who would go by Sam.

In 1927 my grandmother Dussolina died, and Valentino went back to Italy to take care of some land business and find a new wife. He packed Felicia and Santino off with relatives but took my father with him for the trip. By the time they came back to Scranton, six months later, my father had a new mother but also had forgotten a lot of his English, and the kids of the Marvine teased him by calling him "Italiano."

That quickly was shortened to "Tully," and over the years it lost its sting and became his nickname used by all his close friends. Tully is what my mother calls him. It is what I call him.

The original teasing must have had an effect, though, because Tully is one of the most assimilated Italians I know from his generation—a generation that made assimilation its mission. He's kept none of his father's language, with its melody and commedia dell'arte gesturing. His only nod to being a *paisan* is a sweet and buttery tomato sauce he has cooked since I was a kid.

In the seventies, ethnicity became cool again, but by then my father and his siblings had lost most of their Italianness for good. If you put the first-generation Marcheses into a room together they look Italian, but there is none of the stereotypical stuff, the boisterous wine-and-macaroni warmth. They are teetotalers who watch their diets, a dour, shy bunch—"so serious" in the estimation of my mother, the former Rosemary Padden. She comes from a larger, Irish clan, better established though they certainly never reached true lace curtain status. The Padden family had its share of successes and troubles, the troubles always related in some way to the whiskey curse. But in most ways, they are more fun-loving than my father's side. The one exception is his youngest brother, Bastiano Marchese, born of Valentino's second wife, who golfs and buys Cadillacs and drinks beer and is—again, according to my mother—"happy-go-lucky."

I have called my father Tully since I was thirteen or so. It started as a wiseacre teenage thing and just became a habit. "John," he'll say when I pick up the phone, "it's Tully." I already know, because he has a strong Scranton accent, which takes consonants and crushes them to pulp and makes vowels as flat and stretched-out as taffy.

When I moved away from Scranton, I worked for years to rid myself of that accent and by now I've succeeded, unless I get really tired and my guard slips. I've also changed the pronunciation of my name. In Scranton, the family had Americanized it to Mar-*case*. But when I started living in big cities with ethnic enclaves, people knew the correct way to say it, and over time I got in the habit of using "Mar-*kay*-zee." I suppose it is a mixed message I'm sending by using my self-taught radio announcer's voice to pronounce my name in the authentic old-country way. Sometimes I feel as pretentious and pathetic as that kid born in North Dakota as James Gatz, who later became Jay Gatsby and called his phony friends "old sport."

When I started looking for a house, I didn't even consider Scranton. Instead, I had drawn a semicircle on the map with the center being the Delaware Water Gap, a pretty spot on Interstate 80 where the Delaware River divides New Jersey and Pennsylvania. It's about ninety miles from the Lincoln Tunnel and about fifty miles from my father's house in north Scranton. That was as far as I could expect Tully to drive to come and work with me. My radius left a twenty-five-mile buffer zone on the east side of Scranton.

Scranton seems to have revived itself in recent years. There's a palpable feel of life nowadays that was missing when I last lived there, twenty years ago. Still, while there was something about my home that I wanted to know and reconnect with, I knew that I didn't want to actually go home again. Like Kazin's Brooklyn, Scranton was a good place to be *from*. I remember years ago my father saying, "There's nothing here for you." I chose to believe he was still right about that.

I usually drove in from New York on a Tuesday afternoon, racing the rush hour out of town and arriving in Scranton before dark. Leaving New York physically is an analog of escaping it psychically. As I left my street in the East Village, my drive north along the East River on the FDR Drive presented all the horrors of the city in a snaking, high-speed tableau. The dirt, the graffiti, the adamant ugliness of the lower East Side shifted quickly to the smug poshness of a looming Sutton Place and then back again to East Harlem's squalor. Like the city, the road was often hostile, overcrowded, the traffic inching forward, no apparent reason for the delay except that too many people were trying to do the same thing at once, each motorist sealed in his carapace like an angry ant. If the road was open and the traffic flowing, the drivers would race up the side of the East River, performing at sixty-five or seventy miles an hour the jostling contest that takes place at a slower speed on the city's sidewalks. There, even the best-dressed and most fortunate move with the single-minded rudeness and selfishness they believe is necessary for survival in the city. Getting about in New York is the same in any mode and is surprisingly similar in a figurative and literal sense. You can get places here, great places, but unless you're really lucky, the journey is often an unpleasant experience of clawing and weaving.

Invariably, sometime after I'd reached the Harlem River and felt the slight, childish thrill of passing Yankee Stadium, I would think to myself, *I can't wait to get out of this ugly and awful city.* Then, a few minutes later, roaring across the windswept upper lanes of the George Washington Bridge, I would catch a glimpse of the Midtown towers in the afternoon light and feel the familiar rapture, the glory and power and sexiness of New York City, which somehow radiates from those steel-and-stone skyscrapers shining in the sunlight five miles away. "All that glamour and loneliness," Fitzgerald wrote, and I had on occasion felt the caress and sting of both those words. But it seemed that as soon as I was finally free of New York, seeing it in glimpses, I would think, *There isn't a more beautiful city. Where else could I live?*

By the time I'd crossed New Jersey to Pennsylvania, I was back on track. I'd pull into a truckstop on Route 80 and pick up a pile of those real estate guides that are stacked in truck stops and diners around the country. At home, my father was usually waiting with dinner. Since he stopped working construction he has gradually taken on more and more of the cooking for himself, having given up on the idea that my mother would ever use a spice that wasn't salt or pepper. These days they will sit down to dinner, my father behind a platter of sausage and peppers and pasta and my mother carefully picking at noodles with butter. Their habit is to put dinner down around five P.M. and then linger over the table for about twelve minutes, with dessert ready the second the main course is finished.

On my first visits I would try to change their routine. "I usually eat a little bit later," I'd say.

"We can wait until six," my mother would say, trying, as always, to be accommodating.

It didn't matter. All I really wanted to do was get to those real estate brochures.

What was I looking for? I had no clear idea. I had once lived in a duplex apartment with a spiral staircase placed in a garage behind a fake Georgian mansion with weeping willows. I thought that was pretty nice. I'd lived without embarrassment in a series of shabby Philadelphia rowhouses and one gracious brown brick home with a turret and a wraparound porch. The summer before I moved to New York, I was quite content in a ricky-ticky contemporary cabin with lots of glass in odd shapes and a siding called T-111 that looked like someone had tried, unsuccessfully, to imitate wood. I'd occupied what could best be called a yuppie loft in a converted candy factory in Brooklyn. But the only real house I knew was the one I'd grown up in, where I sat now. Like almost everyone who has returned home, I felt claustrophobic here—the house seemed so much smaller than my memories of it. Still, the structure where I sat in middle age was nothing like the place I'd known as a kid. My father had seen to that. Porches had become closets. Hallways had expanded into bedrooms. Bedrooms were altered again into dining rooms. So, in a way, my fundamental idea of what a house was was a thing that kept changing every few years. A house was something you worked on.

In that picture I kept of Tully, the one my mother had labeled "The Hunter," he is standing at the rear of his house, in an enclosed room with carpeting and heat, now his place to watch television and get away from my mother. He is near the doorway to the back bedroom. Neither of those rooms was on the house when I was born. That part of the house sprang from the backyard in 1960, when I was three. My role in building it has provided one of the oft-told stories in the family oral history, the Marchese mythos. That was the year I was spotted as a prodigy.

My talents were revealed when I got my hands on a hammer and nails and scrap pieces of two-by-four that were being used to frame a new bedroom for my parents, who now had two kids and needed more room. The construction turned the house into a mess. Boards were stacked everywhere, and dirt and dust blanketed the floors and counters as if a light gray February snow had fallen. My father worked on this project after he'd put in his regular shift building something else. My grandfather worked on it, too. Often, they were helped by construction worker friends. Those guys had also worked all day, but followed the code that when your buddy had work to do on his house, you helped. They were big guys with loud, rough voices who clomped around the house in heavy shoes, wearing thick leather belts on which hammers hung like six-shooters.

While they worked, I pounded nails into boards—small, short and stubby roofing nails. Even for a child, working with these nails didn't take much skill; their heads were the size of dimes. But I'm told that everyone on the project decided I was showing signs of precocious talent for construction work. I'm sure these cursing and tobacco-chewing guys called me a chip off the old block without much worry that they were indulging in cliché.

In home renovation terms, that bedroom was my father's Mercury Project, a quick, relatively simple test of his own skills, a mission made necessary by his growing family. He was aiming merely for the moon then, though eventually he'd go for Mars. Over the years, he would completely transform this place. Nothing would remain untouched.

He did this despite the fact that he didn't own the house. We rented from my grandfather—my mother's father—who'd been widowed at a young age. For the rest of his life, my grandfather slept in a single bed in an apartment upstairs, and we took over the burgeoning ground floor. My mother's father was a master plumber, as were his brother and one of his two sons. He'd helped my father get started as a laborer in the construction business, though for some reason my father never learned his father-in-law's well-paid trade. To this day, I think my mother feels she married beneath her.

The deed to the house is partly in my father's name now, since my mother inherited the place when her father died. But by then, my father had come to own the place by default, by transforming every inch of space with his own materials, to his own design, accumulating what could only be called sweat equity. Walls were torn out, ceilings were plastered, rooms appeared where there had been grass, windows seemed to move across the walls like shadows. After he renovated the entire house once, he started redoing that back porch he'd built when I was three. This time it got special windows and a stucco wall with ornamental stones blown into it while the plaster was still wet. This was the beginning of what I think of as my father's ornamental stone period. He'd seen this done on some project, and it had seized his imagination. When the porch was finished, he built a dog kennel in the same style. It was an amazing structure, a little canine Astrodome, covered with colored stones about the size of raisins. We teased him that it looked like a World War II pillbox, but our teasing didn't faze him.

I once caught my father standing alone in the kitchen pretending to be an orchestra conductor. But that was the only time he ever showed signs that his artistic impulses weren't fully channeled into his work with plaster or concrete. I remember him standing near that dog kennel wearing an expression of pride that I'd later see in pictures of Picasso in his studio. At one point, I believe, he wanted to cover the entire house in a skin of stones, but my grandfather talked some sense into him.

Building things seemed to be the most natural thing in the world to me. Before I was a teenager, I began to collect plans. I mean that literally: blueprints were stacked around my bedroom. My father brought them home from building sites where he was preparing walls and ceilings to be plastered, doing work which, if done right, would remain invisible. My mother did the cooking in those days, and often after the dinner table was cleared, my father and I would go over these blueprints, stretched out on the kitchen table, smelling of iodine and feeling to the hand like a brittle, dusty rag. Sometimes we'd even get in the car and visit a building my father was working on, and he'd point out the features the architects had designed that made it hard for someone like him to do his job.

I bought grid paper and cheap plastic templates from Woolworth's and spent hours drawing buildings, copying the style I'd seen in the blueprints. At that age, most of my friends were still drawing cars, souped-up hot rods in comic book fashion. I redesigned my bedroom dozens of times, with hidden beds and reading nooks and sleeping lofts and special cabinets for televisions. When there was talk of getting a back-yard pool, I drew a series of plans that turned our quarter-acre plot into the hanging gardens of Babylon. My father was encouraging overall, but the phrase I remember most from our sessions together was, "No, that won't work." If I were to become an architect someday, maybe I wouldn't be one of those dumb college-educated guys who were overpaid and forced workers to make stupid, nearly impossible things.

When I reached the age where I started thinking of what I would do with my life, no one on either side of my family had been to college. The men were plumbers and lathers, machinists and telephone installers, and the women stayed at home. My mother's youngest brother had become a state policeman, and the fact that he'd made it through the train-ing academy was talked about as if he'd been a Rhodes Scholar. Yet there never seemed to be any question that I'd go to college. With the unspoken decision that I would be the first Marchese man to wear a white collar, architecture seemed logical.

It seems self-dramatizing for me even to mention it now, an attempt to make something mundane into something strange and exotic. It's not as if I'd leapt from a family of shepherds or circus acrobats. But since I've left Scranton, almost everyone I've come to know is from the second or third generation of educated people. Many of the folks I work with are second-generation Ivy Leaguers, and most of them, I'll bet, couldn't even name someone their age who didn't attend college. Yet coming back to Scranton, mooning around the old neighborhood, I am reminded that only a few of my childhood friends made it. The three Yanyl brothers across the street followed each other into high-paid and dangerous iron work. Pat Trunzo, the cop's son down the street, went to work in a battery factory and waited until his thirties to go to college. Tommy Zarick joined the air force. My second cousin Donald, son of a steam fitter, became a lawyer. But his two younger brothers never went past high school.

I have eight first cousins, only two of whom are college graduates. In fact, the one-generation leap from lather to architect—blue collar to white—is much harder than it looks. One study I've seen says that only ten percent make it in any generation.

There's a small shelf of memoirs by writers who came of age before World War II—men like Alfred Kazin and Norman Podhoretz—that discuss the sense of dislocation these men felt leaving the immigrant working class and climbing into the white-collar world of dinner parties and book chat. Since the fifties, this social climb has become such an expected part of life that many people forget about the odd, dizzying feeling of floating between two classes. People like me feel forced to disdain the class we've climbed out of. At the same time, we often feel inferior to the class we've joined.

Frank Lentricchia, a working-class kid who is now an English professor at Duke University, wrote about this feeling in a book called *Criticism and Social Change:* "To become an intellectual from this kind of background means typically trying to forget where you've come from." I'm hardly an intellectual—I'm just always reading a book—but the feeling is the same. The essayist Richard Rodriguez, son of Mexican immigrants, perfectly described the orphaned feeling among those of us who try to climb out of our class: "My parents— who are no longer my parents in a cultural sense."

I'm not sure yet whether my parents had the same feeling from their end, whether they thought they were losing my sister and me by giving us everything they could, including license to leave them. Already, my father has started to remind me that he predicted I would one day want to know construction skills, but I think he's inventing a memory. Maybe he never said it out loud, but he might as well have recited the line as he left for work each morning or while he scrubbed the dirt off in the kitchen sink when he came home: *I work with my hands so you won't ever have to.* He never doubted that by fulfilling that promise he would make my life better than his. Not just materially, although that standard is the first he would notice. My sister played it safe. She became a schoolteacher and eventually married a successful lawyer. I have been the black sheep, though my rebellion is ridiculously mild and could be reduced to a single offense: *That Marchese boy broke his parents' hearts. He never became vested in a decent retirement program.* Granted, my father has never understood why I don't just hold on to a decent job with fringe benefits and a 401(k) plan. I always felt I had done the right thing when I quit yet another job to try to make it as a freelance writer. And I always felt like a failure when it came time to tell my family.

When I came home again, I felt like a failure in more ways than one.

5.

Dream House

We had spread out before us on the table the little journals. *Pocono Shopper. Real Estate Marketplace.* They were cheerful documents, full of hope and wonder, "amazing" land packages and you-gotta-see-it-to-believe-it promises. "Country charmer" was a phrase that kept appearing, as if Cary Grant were walking us through the pages. I opened each issue with a feeling that my future would appear before me, and within ten minutes I started getting depressed. "Do you have any Scotch?" I asked my mother. The real work was about to begin—making my dreams fit into a small square box of reality.

My budget was tight. I wanted to pay about $50,000 and then redo the place with another $25,000 for materials and whatever labor we couldn't manage ourselves, which at that time I assumed would be nothing. The Poconos real estate market was hardly booming, but the most amazing thing I learned from these little books was how little $50,000 would get you. From the beginning of the search, my future looked a bit drab and kind of cramped.

We talk about "dream" houses for a very good reason. Seeing a house we like starts up an inner movie of our life lived in it, a daydream that is based only slightly on fact. Over the next four months, as we surveyed somewhere between sixty and seventy-five houses, I played for myself hundreds of scenarios. Typically, they went something like this:

I am sitting in a window seat flooded with light, reading a book in the early morning, sipping my vacuum-sealed, air-shipped, freshly ground coffee. Taking a break from reading— what is it today, a new novel by one of those clever, acerbic Brits?—I pad to the kitchen and stir the stockpot on my six-burner stainless-steel Viking stove. I'm expecting guests for the weekend and there's a new dish I'm working on. I hope the weather will be warm enough to eat on the flagstone terrace.

My father would see the same place and think this:

It's so far back from the road and stuck in the middle of all those goddamn trees that there's no way you're going to get in and out of there in the winter. The filler pipe for the oil tank is around at the back of the house, so while you're stuck in there with a foot of snow, the oil truck will never get close enough to fill the tank and there'll be no heat and the pipes will bust and ruin everything. You'll freeze to death. There's no full base-ment. The crawl space is probably filled with water. The freakin' foundation will collapse eventually, and then you've got a big mess.

We drove around for weeks, looking at cottages and cabins, each one more dilapidated or preposterous than the last. My $50,000 budget kept climbing upward. In a month I was telling realtors that I had a range—up to $75,000. Still we waded through crap. "I wouldn't give you a nickel for that house," my father would say, often. "How much do they want for that?" I'd tell him—again. He'd shake his head. "It's a shack." Sometimes we wouldn't even leave the car. My father could see whatever was wrong from the passenger seat. "It's a catastrophe," he'd say, and I'd push the car back into gear and drive off to the next disappointment.

I had been through this before with my father, and I knew enough to discount some of his negativity. Five years before, I'd invited Mister Worst Case Scenario to inspect a house with me. I'd been driving around the eastern edge of Wayne County, Pennsylvania, one weekend when I came across a one-room schoolhouse in the town of Beach Lake. It had been badly converted to living quarters years before, but it really was, in my eyes, a country charmer, sitting under two spreading maple trees. It had wood siding, a metal roof, a shady, railed front porch, and a big front window trimmed in simple stained-glass squares. The inside was a mess, but I wanted to gut the place anyway. What did I care?

My father came prepared for the inspection with his knuckles. As long as I can remember, he has rapped on walls—in houses, restaurants, anywhere—and gauged the quality of the place by what he hears. I somehow picked up the habit myself, even though I had no idea what he was hitting or what he was listening for. For all I knew, I might as well have circled my thumbs and forefingers, held them to my eyes like fake binoculars, and pretended to judge the tensile strength of the lumber with X-ray vision. But there I would be, rapping away.

"Oh my *Gaad*, John," he'd said, walking into the kitchen of the schoolhouse. "Look at this place." There was cheap paneling everywhere, walls that stopped three feet short of the ceiling, and a floor that sloped like a boat launch. If you dropped a grape in the dining area, you'd have to race it to the bathroom.

Tully walked through, rapping the rap, cursing the construction, damning the previous owners to the special circle of hell where shoddy renovators twist and burn. The real estate agent with us that day was a young guy with a country cockiness in inverse proportion to his sophistication. Watching his commission fade with the old guy's each knock and epithet, he pulled me aside and said, "I think I heard about this inspector you're using. He's supposed to be a real asshole. Where'd you find him?"

"He's my father."

After that the young man went to the car to wait.

When we were finished, I took Tully to an old resort hotel for a drink. As usual, he had a soda—he buys a case of beer at Christmas, and it usually lasts through the next Thanksgiving. We sat in front of a fireplace, and he told me that perhaps the easiest thing to do would be to destroy the house and start over.

"If you want my opinion, I'd take a bulldozer to it."

I didn't want his opinion. I defended the house. How about the stained glass in the front window? What about the solid old lumber that framed the place? (Inspecting the attic, Tully had actually been impressed.) What about the shed in back that would make a great office?

"I think you'd be buying a big mess," he said. "Why not just get a lot and put up a new house?" To people like my father, who have worked around ancient rotting boards and sagging foundations, old is not charming. It's just old.

To explain my aesthetics to him would demand a bridging of those years since I'd left home. I could be impractical because I've never had to clean up a mess. I had become the type of guy who drank expensive coffee and thumbed through shelter magazines. My father had actually built shelter. We finished our drinks, and I drove him back to Scranton and headed home to New York.

I remember feeling nearly nauseated with regret that night. My father had stolen my little dream. And yet how could I argue with him? He knew his stuff, and I knew nothing. I was so depressed I went to bed. Now I'd have to start looking for another place. Maybe my father had no interest in working with me. Maybe he envisioned a project in which he'd do all the awful work and I'd blithely hammer nails into boards like a three-year-old. Maybe the whole thing was a stupid idea.

The next morning, the phone rang early.

"John," said my father, "it's Tully."

"What's up?"

He let out a slightly embarrassed chuckle. "I couldn't sleep all night. I was thinkin' about what we could do with that house."

My God, his change of heart was like a beam of sunshine on a constantly cloudy day. That afternoon I made a bid, but it was rejected, and so were my next two. After a few weeks of phone calls with that young realtor, I finally had to give up on the schoolhouse. Five years later, my father was strapping me into the same emotional roller-coaster ride three or four days a week. And we weren't seeing many places that even came close to that schoolhouse in charm or potential or price. With each shack, I would try to raise a small balloon of hope, and he would pop it. He seemed to have no aesthetics or imagination. Or else, in his mind, form followed so far behind function that he simply could not imagine enjoying a view unless he knew the septic system was in good condition. The French doors of a dining room held no appeal to this man unless he was certain that the walls that held them were plumb.

One day we toured a little stone cottage that had been built sometime in the eighteen hundreds. The joists that held up the first floor were supported by timbers hewn from trees that had seen the Civil War. Inside, someone had put linoleum down, but the kitchen floor was still the original foot-wide rough-hewn planks. I looked at it and saw the boards freshly polished with simple Shaker rugs scattered about and easily imagined a spread in *Country Living* magazine, to which I'd recently taken out a hopeful subscription. My father came up behind me and saw the direction of my stare and said, "Don't worry, we can cover those floors."

"Why? Why would you cover those floors? Those floors are the best thing about this place."

"You're kiddin' me," he said.

We looked at each other for three full beats, and I'm convinced we were thinking the exact same thing: *Excuse me, do I know you?*

We'd been through maybe three dozen houses when I first thought again of giving up. A house in the country was a dream that a single guy without a full-time job probably shouldn't have. The days of Thoreau were long gone. Even factoring in inflation, I couldn't wander out into the woods and build something for the twentieth-century equivalent of twenty-eight dollars and some change. I needed a mortgage and maybe a construction loan. With the prices I was seeing, the bankers would have me spinning out the door as soon as they looked at my tax returns. Then, when the tulips started to push through the defrosting soil, we stumbled onto the firemen's house.

The day had begun as usual. We had planned our visits by looking at the real estate brochures the night before, and in the morning my father had called in to City Hall to tell them that he was "sick." He had accumulated so many unused sick days and put in so much unpaid overtime in the three months he actually had work to do—supervising Scranton's street paving program—that he could never use up the days coming to him. His boss was a high school class-mate of mine. One day when I went into the office to visit my father, my former classmate and I had sat talking for a few minutes and he'd said to me, "I wish you could convince your father to take it easy. He's the oldest guy around here and he's always the first one in the office every morning. And he'll never take time off."

The fact was, Tully didn't have anything else to do. His life had contracted. He went to work, and when he wasn't working he worked around the house, and when he wasn't doing that he was thinking about work or about working around the house. It wasn't any quest for advancement or money that made him like this. He had been in the same low-level job for sixteen years, since he gave up on the vagaries of construction work in a region that seemed to be in permanent recession. The job stress in City Hall was pretty light and in some ways perfect for a guy who was punching a clock nearly a decade past retirement age. But he didn't make much money, and there was little job satisfaction. Worst of all, there wasn't really much work. "Mostly," he would complain, "I sit around with my feet up on the desk." The young people in the office were always gossiping, and he didn't like the language the women used.

During the short weeks of a northeastern Pennsylvania summer, he happily coaxed his backyard into something resembling Augusta National golf course, with the added charms of a concrete lawn jockey and a cherub birdbath. The rest of the year, he was home by four-thirty in the afternoon, when he turned on the Weather Channel and began the trudge down the long dark path to bedtime. If he dreamed at night, it was probably of weather patterns. Sometimes I felt bad for him.

On the day we found the firemen's house, we had looked at a few houses in Stroudsburg, Pennsylvania, which was close to my dream location. For the most part, I was resigned to violating those famously inviolable three laws of real estate (Location, Location, Location) and instead focussing on House, House, House and then Price, Price, Price. It was quickly obvious that I was a few years too late coming to Stroudsburg. The New York commuters (at least those willing to spend two hours traveling each way every day) had already pushed the property values out of my reach. And they were turning it into a town with an urgency about it that didn't seem rural anymore and a feeling of guardedness that comes when a small town turns overnight into a collection of strangers.

But about ten miles away, on winding State Route 191, which runs behind the Poconos' quintessential honeymoon resort, Mount Airy Lodge, we passed a small hand-painted house-for-sale sign with a phone number. Twenty yards back from the road stood a compact, two-story Federal-style house with a sagging porch decked with half-hearted Victorian filigree trim. It was dun-colored and built of man-made blocks cast to look like stone dressed to uniformity by a mason. The roof was slate and brought to mind a word that had yet to pop into my head while touring any other house: "patina."

We made our way around to the back door, and my father bridged his hands over his eyebrows to look in. Then he pushed at the back door, and it sprang open. What the hell? We pushed harder and went in. For the next thirty minutes, I watched my father fall in love.

The rooms were empty except for an orange refrigerator in a corner of the kitchen. It was a true, big country kitchen with wainscoting caked in layers of faded enamel paint. A smaller front room held a short stairway to the second floor. Upstairs were one large bedroom, a tiny bedroom, and a huge bathroom with a clawfoot tub.

"We'll have a hell of a time gettin' rid of that," my father said when he saw the tub.

"Why would we get rid of it?"

"You want that old thing?"

"Yes," I said, with an intonation that is nowadays reserved for the word "duh."

"Suit yourself."

We climbed into the attic and discovered that it was large and high enough to add a bedroom and a bath. The slate roof, though, sat right on top of the roof beams (the previous owner had seen no need for that new-fangled insulation), and spikes of light pierced the rock shingles and stuck in the floorboards. It looked like I would have to sacrifice my patina.

In the basement, the stone foundation was holding up well, but a worn-out hot-air furnace would have to be replaced. There was a small shed stuck on the back wall where a washer had been. The window frames were concrete—there wouldn't be any chance of changing those. All in all, though, there was something about the place that my father thought was just right.

"Now *this* is a house," he said. "Let's call the number."

We drove down the road to an old-fashioned gas station, the kind of place where guys sit around all day and watch the mechanic work, and the only people who actually stop for gas must need it really badly. The owner, it turned out, knew all about the house. His friend had owned it. He'd died recently, having lived there into his nineties (and obviously not having spent a lot of time redecorating). He had willed the house to the local volunteer fire department, and its members were selling it themselves. The asking price was $55,000.

I exchanged a conspiratorial look with my father. "I might be able to come somewhere near that," I said.

"Well, don't matter right now," I was told by the gas station owner and fireman. A sale was pending, already into contract stage. The fire department was waiting for the buyers to get mortgage approval.

"That don't mean nothin'," he said. "We've had a few times where the contract fell through. If you're interested, you should keep in touch."

For the next month, we did nothing but keep in touch. We kept looking at other houses, but it was a formality now. "I have a good feeling about the firemen's house," my father kept saying. Somehow, our roles had switched. He was infatuated with a building, and I was convinced that something would go wrong and it would slip away. "Let's not count on it," I would tell Tully. "Let's keep looking." One night I arrived in Scranton to find him doing neat, precise drawings of the firemen's house, planning how to fit new rooms into the attic, trying to find the right way to reconfigure doorways. "You should see this house, Rose," he would tell my mother. "It's solid." He drove her out to see it. He even came to accept the idea of the clawfoot tub, though he still couldn't understand why I wouldn't just buy a one-piece fiberglass unit and throw the old piece of junk away. "I'm keeping that tub," I'd tell him.

"It'd make a nice planter," he suggested once, which I guess was an attempt at compromise.

Now we rode around the Poconos with less purpose, often visiting houses close to the firemen's house, just so we could drive by and dream. Meanwhile, every road we traveled became Memory Lane. On the old two-lane turnpike that for a short stretch is the main street of the village called Delaware Water Gap, I would remember going to a dowdy roadhouse inn called the Deer Head to hear a wonderful jazz pianist named Johnny Coates. I was sixteen, and it was the first time I'd heard good live jazz in a club. The constituent elements—the hushed attention of the crowd, the melodies flowing from the piano, the alcohol and the smoke—made me feel I had found that great good place. I have spent much time since then trying to play jazz myself, and perhaps even more hours sitting and listening to jazz in clubs that are more expensive and less congenial and somehow never match the feeling of the Deer Head. Twenty-some years after my first visit, I still wanted nothing more than to live nearby.

I remembered another night in the Water Gap. I was on the other side of the short main street, in the back room of a health-food brick-oven pizza parlor (this was the seventies) playing some fledgling jazz with my bass-player friend Tony and a guitarist he had met named Joe Cohn. We had to stop playing when Joe's father came in. He was Al Cohn, the legendary tenor saxophone player, one of Woody Herman's Four Brothers and a soloist who'd made some classic records in the sixties, often with his friend Zoot Sims. Al had stopped in that night to see his son and say good-bye. He was off to the Netherlands to play a job. It was a simple family moment. And yet I told that story for years—*off to the Netherlands to play a job!*—because it made me giddy to think there were people with such huge horizons.

At the same time, of course, it illustrated very well how my childhood horizons were so limited. At that time, I'd never even been on a plane, nor had my father (something he wouldn't change for another twenty-five years, until his grandchildren coaxed him to go to Disney World). By the time I met Al Cohn, I had already decided that architecture was out. Regardless of any obvious signs of talent, what I wanted to do for a living was to become a jazz and studio musician. Why wasn't my father Al Cohn?

The same sort of rolling nostalgia affected my father as we drove through those days. He knew the Poconos in a different way. For me, these hump-backed mountains were mostly a high-speed blur, a pretty place to pass through on the interstate, a stopover on the way back to the city after a progressively rare visit to Scranton for a holiday.

But my father knew the region as he knew other things—at a slower speed. When he married my mother, in 1947, they'd gone there, thirty-five miles on the train, for their honeymoon. Before that, in the months he was waiting to be shipped overseas during the war, he'd hitchhiked home from his base in New York through these same towns—the Water Gap, Stroudsburg, Mount Pocono. His memories of his travels were still surprisingly vivid. It must have been an important and heightened time for him, just twenty years old and heading for the war. Sometimes he would remember the color and make of a car that had picked him up. I imagined him, in the leather seats of those big steel monsters, in his uniform, telling some stranger his life story. On his way home to see his girl. Did he have plans after the war? After marriage? "I've always wanted to do something with my hands," he'd say. He was still saying that fifty years later.

When Tully actually began his adult life and started working with his hands, he often ended up on construction jobs around the area. Now, just about every hamlet held some piece of him. "I worked on that school over there," he'd say as we passed a dowdy, low-rise brick building, whose casement windows and lack of ornamentation were like a sign that read, *This is what passed for architecture in the fifties.*

He'd speculate that the boarded-up ruins of a little motel might be the place where he and his work buddies had stayed overnight when a winter storm trapped them at a construction site. A faded dowager resort, a rambling brick-and-stone pile called Buck Hill, provoked his most distinct recollection of one workday, his version of a memory shared by nearly every modern American of a certain age.

"That's where I was working the day Kennedy was shot," he told me. "We were doing a big renovation there and the news came over the radio and everybody just stopped and nobody did any more work that day." I have my own memory of the same day. Sent home early from school on November 22 to find my mother crying, I thought at first that my father had died. It didn't occur to me that they probably wouldn't close the school just for that.

When Kennedy was killed, my father was almost exactly the same age I am as I write this. A forty-year-old man in the early sixties and a forty-year-old man in the late nineties. Even if we shared the same trade or held identical politics (or taste in bathtubs, for that matter), how could we possibly be the same? How could we talk to each other, except through a filter of misunderstandings, around the distortions of different expectations, the noise that comes of inhabiting worlds in which past, present, and future are so different, and every cultural signpost has changed its meaning?

To my generation, the past is often quaint nostalgia, viewed with a kind of postmodern smirk. Me, I could go through life forgetting decades as if they were house keys. But the Depression haunts my father. "They were really poor," my mother will whisper. "Poor, poor. They didn't have toys. He never got over it." My father likes to tell the story of his two paper routes and how much they meant to him. He is frugal to a degree that is poignant, a guy who will spend half an hour on the phone trying to erase a mistaken charge of twenty-five cents on his long-distance bill. Every time I arrive in Scranton, he can tell me the gas station with the lowest price for regular unleaded.

As a kid, I had taken after the old man and worked a paper route for a short time, but to me the money meant luxuries. We were working class, and while we never had a lot of money, there was always *enough.*

And although my father saw no combat, being part of the Second World War was a big deal for him—duty and responsibility and, maybe most important, glamour. It is still the most glamorous thing he's ever done in his life, crisscrossing the International Date Line on routine patrols aboard a destroyer. It is the only time in his life he's ever left home. Since I became old enough to go to war just after the Vietnam draft was suspended, in 1974, I never even had to register. These differences are hard to see and even more difficult to fathom. And yet they make us so completely different, no matter how much chirpy real estate agents said they could recognize the resemblance between us. Forget it, I wanted to tell them—he is a man who grew up with chickens running around the backyard that became Sunday dinner. I, on the other hand, have found myself in a trendy Chelsea bistro ordering the free-range capon breast.

So now, together, we dreamed our different versions of the same dream. The Firemen's House. We went around like this until a day in May that seemed to hold all the promise of summer, when one of the volunteer firemen called to tell me I couldn't have the house. The buyers ahead of us had secured financing. The deal was done. Finally, I found out why the firemen had been so patient: They were getting the full asking price. The house was sold. Gone.

"Son of a bitch," my father said.

"Well, now we start all over." We'd been shopping for a house nearly full time for three months.

"That would have been a house," my father said.

"It's gone."

"Maybe not."

You're dreamin', I wanted to tell him. But I didn't.

6.

Floyd's House

We took a few days off to wallow in our disappointment, and then hit the road again. During the first week of the renewed search, we moved into new territory—Wayne County—on a road that I had traveled so often that I could feel the curves before they came. As a kid, I'd come this way nearly every winter weekend, learning to ski at a little rope-tow hill with Uncle Santino. For about a year after I dropped out of music school, I'd driven this road two or three nights a week, getting to a honeymoon resort where I played trumpet with the house band. It was early summer now, and in the humid half chill of morning we passed through a pocket of air that carried the scent of mowed grass, that fresh and earthy aroma that mingles growth with decay. I was hit by a Proustian wave of memory —the sort that only smell can trigger. This was not nearly where I *wanted* to live, but the smell was so familiar and welcoming. Something about it made me feel that we were at least heading in the right direction.

We finally stopped in the town of Narrowsburg, New York. It is a hamlet of five hundred people whose main industry is the rental of canoes and rafts to boozy weekend adventurers. The town sits beside a deep and still part of the Delaware River. As we rolled across the metal bridge that carries a two-lane state road from Wayne County, Pennsylvania, into Sullivan County, New York, I suddenly felt another jab of memory.

In the summer after graduating from high school, three of my good friends since grade school and I organized a canoeing and camping trip here. Knowing we all were heading to college and that we were the kind of kids who left Scranton, this seemed like our last chance to hang out before separating, maybe forever. It was also an excuse to sit on a river in the sun and drink beer. (In those days, New York had more lenient drinking laws.) The trip came to a quick conclusion when we damaged a canoe early on the first day and heavy rains rolled in by evening. We never really achieved the great good fellow bonding session, although I do remember drinking a fair bit of beer. After that, the four of us headed off in different directions, and in the twenty-five years since then I have seen those friends rarely. Because of those few soggy days in June, however, Narrowsburg would always seem to me a town for unmet expectations—even slight disappointment—and its weather perfectly normal on a gray rainy afternoon.

On the town's block-long Main Street I met Bill Reiger, whom I call Reiger the Realtor. He's a boisterous bear of a man who was raised just upriver. He turned out to be the first real estate agent who really understood what I was looking for. On our first meeting he showed me four potential houses in my price range, and two looked good enough to bring my father for a second visit. We met Bill and then headed out of town on Route 97, the "scenic highway" that parallels the Delaware River from the New Jersey border in Port Jervis to Hancock, where New York State begins to climb over the top of Pennsylvania. Three miles north of town was the house that I will probably always call "Floyd's Old Place," though now it is mine. I have a feeling everyone in town will always call it Floyd's Old Place.

This was a house that was plain and simple: a one-and-a-half-story Cape Cod. Four rooms downstairs, two up, three closets total, none with doors. Cape Cod houses get their name from the bent-elbow peninsula off the New England coast—from a time when it was a place that possessed a hard-scrabble, frugal modesty, before it became the posh playground it is now. This was the ultimate starter house, which seemed to suit me. I was starting *something*, after all.

According to Reiger the Realtor, this was a starter house for Floyd Campfield, a well-known local character, who'd built it largely himself after he'd gotten out of the army and moved back home. His grandfather had given him the land. Four kids had been born in this tiny place before Floyd moved everyone into larger quarters a half mile up the road.

Over the years, very little was done to improve the place—linoleum here, some cheap plywood paneling there. One of the owners had been talked into installing a cloak of aluminum siding, probably with that promise that the house would never again need a paint job. That was a complete lie, of course. The paint coating the aluminum was scarred and faded, as if it had been blasted by sand. In places, it peeled off in leprous hunks.

Yet through the grime and dowdiness, I could feel something. This was a clean slate of a house, one to which I could do as much or as little as I wanted. It required no grand gestures, no large imagination, but it could easily accept a bold stroke or a flight of fancy. The more I thought about it, the more it seemed I had something in common with this house. We were just about the same age, both of us plain but solid, lived in and a little beaten up, and at that point, empty for a while.

What would my father think? We started in the basement. In the months we had looked at houses, we had almost always started in the basement. In scores of inspections, we'd yet to look at a place that satisfied my father's base requirements. His personal building code had two fundamental rules. The foundation must remain perfectly dry and be built to withstand a nuclear attack.

"You can't go back and fix a foundation," he said again and again as we searched. "But if you got a good foundation, you can build from there." Not bad as mottoes go.

This little house was built on top of poured concrete, eight inches thick, not a substantial crack in sight. It was absolutely dry—almost a first in our travels.

"This is a well-built place," Tully whispered, trying not to let Reiger the Realtor hear him. "We could do something with this place. Anything we did would improve it."

Over the months we'd spent searching, I'd started to see a pattern in my father's choices, a logic for deciding between his few favorites and the many houses he hated. I realized there was more than a bit of self-interest in his standards. It was self-preservation really, though he wouldn't have admitted it. The truth was, he didn't feel up for a back-breaking major renovation, jacking up foundations and digging new floors from the rocky earth. How could I hold this against him? He had turned seventy-three as we searched. "I wish you had decided to do this ten years ago," he told me once.

As we left the house and walked toward the car, my father and I paused to stare up at the huge satellite dish that pointed toward Pennsylvania. It was twelve feet in diameter and made of aluminum. It looked big enough to link me with the more distant planets in our solar system. I had just gone through one of my periodic bouts of resolve to stop watching TV and try to read some of those thousands of books I'd missed. What the hell was I going to do with this behemoth?

"Does that thing work?" I asked Reiger the Realtor.

"Sure does," he said.

We stared at the dish for a while, bending our necks forty degrees and lifting our faces into the sunny sky. Finally, my father turned and said matter of factly, "We could make a gazebo out of it." I knew he was hooked.

We looked at a few other places that day, but driving back to Scranton that evening, my father said, "I think you should go for that Cape Cod." I did. Within a week, we had a deal. I offered the exact amount I had in mind when I first drove across the George Washington Bridge months before—$50,000. The owners wanted a lot more, but I moved up only a little. They had put the house on the market at $69,900. I felt a little bad for them. The husband had been transferred out of the area at the depth of a market slump and had tried renting the place while he waited for a sale. The house sat on the market and empty for several years. I knew I didn't need to be generous, but I didn't think I should try to steal it.

One thing still needed doing before we signed the papers. My father wanted his friend Donny Scartelli to come in and inspect the place, just for a second opinion.

Donny is the guy I might have been. He is a few years younger than I am, taller and better-looking, with the noticeable strength of someone who has done hard physical work his entire life. The day I met Donny, I could, as a result of long years of lonely, obsessive exercise, run ten or twelve miles. I could bench press my weight. But Donny looked as if he could run me down and break me in half.

He wasn't the type, though. His father had come out of the construction trades and started a contracting business, so Donny had learned the dirty grunt work but also had crossed the line into management, handling estimates and negotiations. He exuded the kind of confidence that comes from knowing that you're as smart as anyone else (even if you haven't read a lot of books) and that you are competent enough to deal with all the physical problems of life—repair the faucets, fix the wiring. On the ride to Narrowsburg, Donny talked of the house he was planning to build for himself someday. It will be an impressive place.

My father had taught Donny his trade—lathing—some years before, when Donnie was coming up through an apprentice program sponsored by the trade unions. They had worked together a little bit after that and had lots of contact when my father was covering the city's interests in the building of a $100 million downtown shopping mall in Scranton and the Scartelli firm was hired to do some subcontracting work. There was a rapport between them that made me feel a little jealous. They had shared something that my father and I never had: a day-to-day closeness and a sense of working together as peers. Their ease with each other, despite a forty-year gap in age, was a little bit like mine with some of the older musicians I performed with in big bands. Unlike my father and me, Tully and Donny actually had something in common.

Donny called my father John. *John.* It sounded so familiar, so intimate and friendly. Despite the fact that I called my father by his nickname, by now it had become formalized. I might as well have called him sir. Who was this John? As we drove and he and Donny did most of the talking, I realized that my father was a guy who could joke around, who could gossip about people and curse them behind their backs, do all sorts of things that I'd never seen him do. He asked Donny about his girlfriend. Since I'd broken up with the woman in New York, my parents treated me as if I'd joined a monastery, that girls were something I'd left behind in a previous life.

In the car with Donny, I felt what my parents must feel when I am in their house and I call friends on the telephone. (Because they never liked to visit the city, they have rarely seen me among my friends as an adult.) At home with them,

I am usually tightlipped and reserved. We have our well-worn routines in which we tease one another, but I'd virtually given up trying to joke around; they never seemed to get my references. I would yack away long distance, and they would sit and pretend not to listen. Sometimes I would look at them and see them wondering why I was such a different person on the phone.

Here was my father yacking away with Donnie, someone my own age. It was good to see that he had it in him. But why didn't he have it in him with me?

We drove across the Narrowsburg bridge into New York State. "This is a nice little town," Donny said. We picked up Reiger the Realtor, and in a few minutes, we were at the house. As before, we immediately headed for the basement. Donny didn't rap his knuckles on the walls, but he surveyed everything with a quick, no-nonsense look. Immediately, he saw that the main support beam, made of four two-by-eights spiked together, had sagged. "These should have been two-by-tens—at least," Donny said. He started talking about stuff that I didn't understand at all—J-channels and welding supports. Reiger the Realtor so far had been conspicuously friendly and accommodating, but he began to get defensive.

"Are you an engineer?" he asked Donny tartly.

Donny gave him a hard look. "You don't need to be an engineer to see that. I build things every day of my life." Then Donny told him the floor joists were inadequate and would have to be strengthened. In the attic, Donny was quick to notice what we already knew: The house had been infiltrated by squirrels, who'd made a playground, feeding station, and litter box out of the original fiberglass insulation.

Only a little bit of the destruction was visible in the crawl space. Once we tore down the bedroom ceilings, who knew what we would discover?

"There's some big problems here," Donny kept saying. The realtor did his best at damage control. But Tully and Donny ganged up on him. My father would chip in with even more potential problems. What about the septic system? What about the well? That heater was sitting too close to the floor. There was an oil tank buried in the front yard that was an environmental disaster just waiting to happen. We'd have to replace that. I kept quiet and listened. With all the dire predictions, I began to worry that I was buying a nightmare house—a catastrophe.

Things were tense when we parted from Reiger and headed back toward Scranton. I felt that maybe I'd lost another dream house.

In the car again, we chatted about other subjects for a while. Finally, Donny said, "You should try to get at least twenty-five hundred off the price. It'll cost you at least that much to fix all those things.

"I was being a stickler back there," Donny added. "That's what I figured I should do. But even if you get that house for fifty-one thousand, you're stealing it. That's a good little house."

It took a few difficult phone calls back and forth with Reiger the Realtor to close the deal. The owners agreed to reimburse me for the cost of replacing the buried oil tank. I agreed to hold the price.

So now we were partners in crime, my father and I. We'd spent dozens of days on the road together. The hours had worn some of the edges from each of us. But the real work lay ahead.

The day of the inspection, Donny took us back to his contracting headquarters to show us where we could get those J-channels to fix the sagging main beam. The three of us climbed a long stairway to his office, Donny in the lead, then Tully, then me. Following my father, I noticed that the back of his blue jeans sagged from his butt, and he seemed to labor up the stairs on legs that were skinny and out of proportion to his torso. He gripped the railing hard and seemed to be pulling himself along. For a moment, I thought I might have to help him.

It was the first time in the many hours we'd spent together over the past months—the first time in my life, really—that I realized I was walking behind an old man.

7.

My House

When my father looks at the renovated place now, often he'll say, "This house looks like a million bucks." I wish.

His appraisal is high by a factor of ten or so. But I'll allow some inflation because I know his stake in the house is beyond a measurement I can make, certainly beyond dollars. When we found it, the house looked as plain as a box for cheap cigars. Neglect had made it seem forlorn and destitute. Compared to then, it does look like a million bucks.

When it was built, this kind of house was still the dream home of most Americans. The Cape Cod. I love the style— simple, economical, expandable, and, in its unadorned way, beautiful. Now we live in an era of McMansions—overdressed behemoths that scar suburban hillsides, inhabited by over-achievers flaunting their crass presumption. But in simpler days, it was the Cape Cod that opened its doors and welcomed young couples looking to start their lives. In any given year from the seventeen hundreds until the final greed-crazed decades of the twentieth century, when Americans looked at a Cape Cod, they thought of home. More than a hundred years ago, Henry David Thoreau called the Cape style a "sober-looking place." As we began our renovation, that description seemed fine with me. I felt I could use a little sobriety.

My sober-looking place is a rectangular box, some thirty feet long and twenty-four feet wide. The box is divided into four rooms and a bath on the first floor. The rooms are small but not cramped; they have the diminutive elegance of a nest. Windows dot each wall in a pattern that is symmetrical, but not exactly symmetrical. The front door sits nearly dead center, and to its right is the one concession to ostentation that the builders allowed themselves: a picture window as big as a Ping-Pong table.

On the second floor, where the angles of the roof drop the ceilings down to touchable levels, there are two bedrooms and a couple of makeshift closets. Neither has a door. When I first walked upstairs and into the smaller bedroom, the sight made me catch my breath. The room was lined completely with thickly varnished knotty pine. All that shiny wood, the knots sticking out like eyeballs, was a strange combination of cozy and ominous. This bedroom would lull me into a sleep filled with fitful dreams.

. . .

There are some things I know about the place now, after two years of work, that I couldn't have told you then, during the days when I decided that it would become my house, my first home. There are things you can come to know only by living in a house, and then there are many more small secrets that reveal themselves only to someone who has ripped the place apart and put it back together again.

The roof beams in the ceiling are Douglas fir, two-by-six, and where they join the long east and west walls there are cuts in the beams that are called birdsmouths. There, the beams extend beyond the walls for a few more feet, giving the roof a little more room to run the rain away from the building. The floors are tongue-in-groove yellow pine, mostly, and when you attack them with a sanding machine they seem to warm to the trauma and give off a soft, pale, golden glow. With a new coat of polyurethane, they gleam.

The original windows were made in a mill only four miles down the road, in a part of town called The Flats. The Flats hug the shoreline at a spot called the big eddy, where the Delaware River twists like a snake and begins to straighten out again, a wide slow turn where the river takes a breath and then plunges again toward the Chesapeake Bay. In the nineteenth century, logs were floated down the river to the big cities, and Narrowsburg's big eddy supplied a resting stop for the men who rode the log flotillas. In the twentieth century, Narrowsburg Lumber Company opened a mill on The Flats. The doors of my rooms were probably framed in that mill, too, in the years after the Korean War, the frostiest time of the Cold War. When local guys like Floyd Campfield came home from their obligatory military service, the mill was one of the few places they could find work. Floyd eventually became a policeman, but he was practical and thrifty enough to build his first home while he was an employee of the lumber company. The mill is closed now, and to replace the house's windows I had to drive an hour to a home-renovation supermarket and load machined replacements made in Minnesota. One of my new doors came from Mexico. "Jesus Christ," my father said when he saw the label. "Can't they make *anything* in America anymore?"

My kitchen might have been made in the mill on The Flats, too. But more likely somebody built it in place, cutting plywood with a saw and using a router to make blocks of wood look like cupboard doors. Over the sink was a little decorative piece of pine whose bottom was outlined by a series of moons and stars. The artisan had cut the piece of trim in alternating half circles and triangles, and the homemade look of it was both charming and pathetic. It had to go.

Lots of things had to go. Renovating this house required a daily act of triage, deciding what could be saved, what would be buried out back. If you're not comfortable making choices, I've learned, don't fix a house. Or at least be prepared to be uncomfortable all the time.

The decisions dovetailed and multiplied. The old countertop was a piece of particleboard with the backsplash and bullnose molded right in, covered in a plastic laminate printed to look like butcher block. As renovation progressed, this counter suffered a series of amputations as we made room for new pipes or squarer walls. "You could keep this," my father kept saying. "It's in good shape."

"I don't think so," I told him.

Of course, a new counter made new cabinets a necessity. My new kitchen cabinets are made of the same amalgam of sawdust and glue as the old kitchen counter, only tarted up with a coating of shiny white foil. My father might look at them and say they look like a few thousand bucks, which is about what they cost. I have held each one in place, my legs spread, my arms wide, a blue-jeaned, grunting Atlas, while Tully screwed them to the walls. I caulked the seams between cabinets to hide our small mistakes. I now know what a huge hassle it is to get the hinges on these cursed things to sit square and swing freely.

I would have liked real wood cabinets, of course, but with my budget I'd have been dreaming. Another thing I learned during our renovation is that I have little trouble taking after my father when it comes to frugality. Frugal is a kind, old-fashioned word for it though. Really, you could call us cheap.

This was a cheap house from the beginning. It was built for not much more than I paid merely to have all the bankers and lawyers pass the ownership papers back and forth. But it was built by hand. And it was built by someone who would walk through the finished front door and actually live in the place. It is a noble undertaking, building your own house, and one that reveals a lot about the builder. I would learn that every cut Floyd made seemed to cut two ways. Your strengths and your flaws get built right in.

As I persist in looking for some meaning in this project, I realize that a house can become a metaphor for your life. It reflects not just who you are, but who you think you are and who you want to be. And I realize that the habits of choice you bring with you to a house will shape what you do with it. The wood and the stone and the wires and the glass stand ready to be changed, but it may be the builder who requires the greater renovation. At least that's how it was with me.

8.

Working

I had never worked a day in my life.

How was it possible? A working-class kid from a blue-collar family gets through four decades of living without putting in one full day of paid labor. Had I betrayed my class, or was I proof of its promise? I'm talking about labor in the way it is measured by people who actually work—valuable and substantial in direct relation to the dirt and soreness accumulated by the end of the day.

Sometimes it seems that my earliest memories are filled with fantastic tales of dirt, that my forebears were Paul Bunyans of grime. My father's father, Valentino, the coal miner, was reputed to have had his features turned black with coal dust each workday, to have come home to perform heroic ablutions, to have medicated and narcotized himself with a nightly bottle of homemade wine, only to rise with the sun and descend once again to the blackness of the mine tunnel, a subterranean Sisyphus.

My mother's father, James Padden, the plumber, spent the better part of his waking life wading through other people's excrement (the way I heard it) and would drag himself out of the sordid pits, peel off his soiled clothing, and drop the pile down the clothes chute for my mother to wash. ("They call me the Irish washerwoman," she tells people cheerfully these days. But could it have been joyful work when she was a young mother living in a cramped apartment downstairs from her widowed father?) Later, through his political connections, my grandfather became the city's plumbing inspector, and wore a jacket and tie and kept himself neat and impeccably clean down to his big false teeth. He always smelled like a Hall's Mentholyptus cough drop.

My father, improving his lot, was more often just a dusty man, someone who after the work whistle blew looked as if he'd been smudged, or rolled in gray flour. His head would be filled with fine dirt, and his cleaning rituals were in good part nasal, something that disgusted my mother. He worked many times with asbestos as if it were plaster of Paris. It's a wonder he can still breathe.

And here I am, a white-collar Fauntleroy, a boy whose childhood highlights in the family mythos (and in my own) mostly revolve around costumes. Clean costumes. After that short stint hammering nails on the addition my father built, my construction days were over. I became Roy Rogers for a long time, wearing the same fringed cowboy outfit every day—the washerwoman could clean it only as I slept—and rocking on a wooden Palomino hobby horse until the two-inch springs creaked. "Dale," I would call when I needed something from my mother. There was a period when, inspired by some Disney movie about a child Sherlock Holmes, I went around with a houndstooth fedora with a jaunty green feather stuck on my head and—could it be?—wore an ascot. Getting a rusty brown Nehru jacket was a big event in my youth. My sister will never let me forget that I once told her my dream was to become a male model.

Was I a sissy? I don't think so. I played army with the boys, went in for sports, including bruising games of unpadded tackle football. At the right time, I liked girls. But when it came time to work, the work of my family, of my neighbors, of my class, I just wasn't there. "You weren't interested," my father reminds me. "You wanted to play baseball, or play your trumpet." I think now that I just didn't want to get dirty.

As an adult, I have met many men from the upper middle class. Talking to them, I've often heard stories of a short period of hard work in their past, a voyeuristic expedition into the sensual world of manual labor. Summers in forests sawing down trees, sweaty months in the Southwest pounding nails for some fly-by-night nonunion developer, a smelly cruise on a commercial fishing boat. They might have known the Oscar Wilde line—"There is nothing necessarily dignified about manual labor, and most of it is absolutely degrading"—but they had to prove it to themselves.

I didn't. Consequently, my work during summer vacations sounds like the pathetic monologue of some gin-soaked has-been advertising man you'd meet in a has-been New York bar. *That year, I ended up as the puppeteer for a children's television program called Magic Window. There wasn't much magic involved—I made most of the puppets myself.... That summer, I did my best pretending to be a police reporter out there on the Texas Panhandle. Let me tell you, I didn't fool those good ol' boy Texas Rangers for one minute.... Those were the days when bands had horns in them, and we played everything—dance sets, comics, singers, belly dancers. There was this one who went by name Phaedra, but her real name was Doris and* ... Check, please.

Now, my thirty-ninth birthday arrives and I am a home-owner, but not yet a resident. I throw a party in Manhattan, and the menu is filled with buffala mozzarella and fresh pesto and wine and booze and publishing gossip of all sorts. It is a last hurrah for my old life. There are book people, magazine people, a first-time author from across the street. My literary agent calls to say he's sorry he can't make it. Soon, I greet newcomers at the elevator with a leather tool belt friends have bought me, a bottle of Scotch stuffed in one pocket, a bottle of gin in another, and a corkscrew in the hammer loop. At two in the morning, barely able to stand straight, I am playing "Moonlight in Vermont" with a jazz trio, sitting in at a smoke-saturated little East Village club. A woman I have known for years decides we should spend the night together. Happy birthday to me. It is the Lost Weekend. When the weekend is over, I start my new life of work.

. . .

Monday morning, the first fresh September day heralding fall, and I lift myself from a thin futon thrown on the floor of my house and feel anxious. My father is on his way. I have to decide what to wear.

He arrives minutes past nine. He has left his house, I know for certain, at exactly eight o'clock, and will from now on leave nearly always at exactly eight o'clock. There will be no rushing involved. He will be ready to leave at seven-thirty, maybe even seven. Then he will cool his heels. He will make the drive a few hundred times, and each trip he will clock to the minute.

The morning air is chilled, and a thin opaque fog rises off the Delaware River, climbs the few hundred yards up the slope toward my house, obscuring the branches lower down and crawling among the tree trunks in my backyard like a dry-ice movie mist. But the day will be warm eventually, and I have decided to dress in cotton. It's my latest costume. My pants are a green fatigue color, purchased from the Banana Republic at the lower end of Greenwich Village. My shirt is white and oddly cut, with a pointed collar and big, wide body. I got two of them from a formerly chic, now defunct shop in Soho. Counting last season's running shoes, I am wearing nearly three hundred dollars' worth of old clothes. For some reason, I can't resist mentioning this to my father, and when I do his head snaps back a few inches and the only thing he can say is, "You gotta' be kiddin' me."

Tully wears one of the two pairs of pants he owns that still fit him, dungarees that my mother bought him from Sears. On top, a gray sweatshirt, heavy on the polyester, spotted and stained from many things, mostly the tobacco that he chews. For the drive he is wearing sneakers with Velcro tabs. He will buy them only when they go on sale for less than ten bucks. Soon after he arrives, he changes into a pair of Hush Puppies that look like something you'd see dead on the road. He walks on the insides of his feet, and the heels of his shoes are worn into wedges.

Though now firmly into his seventies, my father takes great pride in still being able to bend briskly and touch his toes. It is pretty impressive, considering it has been some decades now since he's been able to stand straight, look down, and actually see them.

I had always presumed that a prodigious belly came with construction work, that guys like my father spent their youth being one kind of hunk and then their middle years truly growing into the word. Tully is olive skinned and dark eyed; I am the opposite. The only direct genetic connection I can trace to him is this belly. For a time in my twenties, my stomach just popped out after a few years of living with a woman who enjoyed fettuccini Alfredo and wine almost as much as I did. It was startling when a friend I hadn't seen in years cornered me in the supermarket and said, "Man, how'd you get so *round?*" I have been in training ever since, but I fear that there is a ticking time bomb of DNA somewhere in my midsection and if I let down my guard for a minute it will explode and I will assume my legacy of girth.

Already, I sense renewed danger. My new life forces me to abandon my posh urban lifestyle. I have resigned my membership in the fancy health and racquet club in Greenwich Village (for years, it was pictured on TV—the club that

Jerry Seinfeld used). There, I paid some company to let me sweat in a converted town house where the price tag for the new terrazzo tile and Corian counters in the shower room easily topped my yearly income. I'm betting that I've devised a clever substitute, buying this fixer-upper.

"So," my father says, taking a last look at my ridiculous outfit. "You ready to work?"

I thought I was. But for the next six weeks, my father beats my expensively aerobicized body into the ground. He has never belonged to a pricey health or racquet club. He is on blood-pressure medication and three different kinds of cholesterol pills. The veins in his legs have decided they would rather be on the outside—standing in shorts, he looks like the Pompidou Center. But he is relentless, and no matter the job, he seems to do most of the actual labor. Partly, he just can't help himself. Partly, I soon realize, he believes that if his life depended on his only son's driving a nail straight— well, he'd rather not have to consider that option.

"I'll get it," he says, as I try a third time to put a three-inch wood screw into the two-by-four-and-plywood bed frame we are building for my futon. Tully cannot conceive of someone sleeping on the floor, so the bed has become our first project. Neither can he conceive of me being competent enough to hold the screw gun correctly, or to set the screw in the proper way, or even to realize that when a couple of two-by-fours are placed together, the first screw should go where they meet. He jabs his finger in the obvious spot and taps it three times, signaling where I should drive the screw.

I hesitate in order to give him an ironic, knowing look, a look that will ask him, *Do you think I am a total idiot?*

"Go ahead," he says impatiently. "Put it here." He taps again. He hasn't heard my silent question, but I've gotten his answer.

I press the dangling screw tip into the wood, and it folds itself off the drill bit and falls to the wooden deck where we're working.

"I'll do it," he says.

"*I'll* do it," I say.

"Okay, but get it right this time."

I don't.

A realization hits me and leaves me slightly stunned. I'm not just making my bed, I'm going to have to lie in it.

I had forgotten some things about my father. He is a man who has a way of doing things. *His* way. The importance of the particular technique is often wholly out of proportion to the importance of the thing being done. For instance, an extension cord is coiled in a series of overlapping loops that are then tied with three turns of the cord around the coil, and the cord is hung on a nail, never laid down. He sees me wind up a twenty-foot orange extension cord in the way I have learned to coil microphone cords—looped around your forearm, palm to elbow—and when I am done, he takes it apart and redoes it his way, making bow-like loops on the floor. Likewise, when a hose is used, it must be put back with one type of connection on the bottom and another on top. I can never remember which is which. Cleaning the basement of the previous owners' junk fills a bunch of heavy green trash bags, and of course there is a specific way that a trash bag should be packed and a right way to twist the neck and release the air so that the bag is full but not ballooned. Tully's bags look like prunes, not plums. But accomplishing that means inhaling most of the fine dust from inside the bag that flies out with the trapped air, and I just don't see the point of it. Consequently, when I get done tying up a trash bag it looks as if it could fly in Macy's Thanksgiving parade. "You know," he says, "if you were an apprentice you'd get yelled at."

Early in October, we are patching the cement edges where the walls meet the floor around the perimeter of my basement. In a five-gallon plastic bucket, I am mixing mortar and water with a small trowel.

"Who taught you how to mix cement?" my father asks. Clearly he does not mean I am doing it in a new and wonderful way that he'd like to learn himself. A splatter of sticky gray mud flies up onto my cheek.

"See," he says, "you gotta get the trowel down into it."

He grabs the tool from my hand and leans over the bucket and starts to mix. He begins his explication—"When a professional mixes it, every drop stays"—and a big glob of the stuff hits him in the nose. Although it is a modern gesture I detest, it is all I can do to stop myself from pumping my fist in the air and yelling, "Yesssss!" Tully clumsily wipes his face and passes the bucket back to me.

I look at the smudge on his nose in triumph. "I guess even professionals screw up sometimes, huh?"

My father says nothing. He loads a trowel with a heap of my inferior mud, takes it to the wall that needs a patch, and spreads it for a while in silence.

Because I have bought a house that essentially needs nothing, renovating means I can repair everything. I have begun making lists, and they immediately spawn other lists, and they multipy, virus-like. Painting the basement walls with coats of sticky waterproof paint has made patching the concrete floors seem necessary. When the basement walls are bright white and the floor looks good, the stairs to the first floor seem torn up and shabby. A few of the steps have been attacked by a former resident canine, and they are mottled with toothmarks. So we buy some two-by-tens to serve as new treads.

Making stairs is a complicated task. You must figure out the distance of the diagonal drop and then determine the ideal number of steps to divide up the length. Then, the steps must be placed at an ideal footfall distance from one another. Drawing plans involves a lot of triangles, which pile up on one another, and one misplaced line can throw the whole thing off. There are tales of angry carpenters placing one stair an inch too low so that the homeowner will trip every day of his life for twenty years. There's an art to this project: it's a job for a Duchamp with a tool belt.

Because his trade became nearly obsolete, my father's last days as a full-time construction worker were spent as a member of the carpenters union. Just the same, carpentry is not really his strength. For our staircase job, he often stops for a long time just to look at things, a stubby pencil behind his ear. Around his neck he has hung his magnifying glasses, bought from one of those revolving racks in some Woolworth's, and every now and then he'll peer birdlike through the thick lenses and scrawl a series of intersecting lines on the back of a clean, slightly sappy piece of new pine. There is a specific nail on my sagging main basement beam where he hangs those glasses at the end of each day, and I've taken to secretly washing them every now and then before the accumulation of sawdust and tobacco juice becomes impasto. Since he never notices that they are dirty, he never notices that they are clean.

The bottom step goes in fine, and the top step falls into place. Now there are two ten-foot-long diagonal boards running from the first floor landing to the concrete floor of the basement. But there's nothing between them, and my father has spent most of the day trying to figure out where to put the rest of the steps. He's getting impatient. He draws some more impromptu plans, but after a moment he stops and slams down the pencil. "I lost my geometry," he says.

Unfortunately, I never had much geometry to begin with. It was the one class I ever flunked in high school, and partly because of that failure, I decided architecture should not be my career. We quit working for the day, leaving me with the equivalent of a diving platform as my way into the basement. But the next morning I prod my father along, and by the end of the day we have placed nine more new stair treads, though, again, Tully has done almost all the work. "Is that okay, boss?" he says, driving the last screw into the last step, having decided I was unequal to this project.

"I thought I was the apprentice," I say.

"You *are* the apprentice. But you dress like the boss."

Fall has made the days dry and cool, and in the middle of October we move outdoors. My property covers just less than three and a half acres and is shaped like a tetrahedron. (I think that's what those geometry guys call it.) It comes to a sharp point on the north side. The house is placed, for some reason, near the tip of that point. If I walk out my kitchen door and step off twenty paces, I am on my neighbor's land. I covet my neighbor's land. It is filled with conifers and dry-laid, mossy stone walls and runs down in a shaded gulley from the road to a pond about the size of a tennis court. The pond was one of the things that made me decide to buy this place. I knew from the beginning I didn't own the water, but I bet it would probably always be there, shining out beyond my kitchen and dining room windows, reflecting the sky and acting as my personal weather report each morning when I woke in the upstairs room I planned as the bedroom. Below the pond is a white-sided eleven-room former boarding house that has been empty of people since I've moved in. My realtor told me that it belonged to a guy named Phillip and his friend Raymond. He said the word "friend" with an exaggerated emphasis and a bit of a wink. The friends have moved into a new house right on the river. Tully and Santino were exploring on the private dirt roads by the river one day, and Phillip blocked their path and introduced himself.

"He's one of *those* guys, I think," my uncle reported later.

"That's what I heard," I said. "I guess I should try to find him one of these days and say hello."

"Don't worry," my father said. "He'll probably find *you.*"

He hasn't yet. We begin at the edge of Phillip's land and start cutting things. My father and uncle each have come armed with weed whackers. Together, with their whack-ers, they look like a geriatric gardening crew from some eccentric estate.

Santino has decided that he will join us one day each week. He retired a few years ago after working many years as a machinist in the same plant that stamped out the grilles for air conditioners. He is as clean and precise at work as his older brother is rough and dirty, and he loves to tackle tedious tasks. He is a quiet man. We once drove together all the way from Dallas to Scranton. There were long stretches during which the conversation consisted solely of Santino musing on road signs: "Nashville." An hour of silence. "Knoxville." And so on. Neither he nor Bastiano nor Felicia ever married, and forty years ago they formed a household together which holds today, as eccentric as the living arrangements in Anne Tyler's *The Accidental Tourist* but as normal as toast to me. As their only nephew, I've been as spoiled as a boy could be.

On our first day of landscaping, my coworkers brought me an implement that is decidedly low-tech—a sickle-like thing about the size of a minature golf club—and some pruning shears. We work through a half-moon-shaped swath of land behind the house, clearing toward the tree line on the ridge fifty yards behind my back window, just beyond which the bottom falls out of the land and it drops toward the flood plain of the river.

When Floyd Campfield decided to build on this lot in the late fifties, he had to truck in tons of rocks and earth to make a level spot near the road for a foundation. The land had been logged, so it was clear—the big old pine trees that I admired when I first spotted the house actually belong to Phillip and Raymond. Like the pond, they are close to my house and mine to look at—squatter's sight rights. Floyd planted a few trees after he finished the house, and these are now forty years along. At the turnoff to my driveway is a straight fir that juts into the sky like a prickly arrow. "I remember being able to jump over that tree when I was a kid," Floyd's eldest son would tell me one day. Although the tree is fifty feet tall, I wouldn't necessarily bet against Floyd Junior on a second attempt.

The information that has been dribbling in on the Campfield family, the homesteaders of my personal frontier, indicates they were a colorful bunch. Behind the house is a solid red oak with crusty gray bark, and sitting next to it is a six-foot-tall stump that might have been its twin. Another Campfield kid had done something Floyd Senior didn't like, and when he tried to escape up that tree, his father started chopping it down out from under him. When Floyd lived here, he hung his deer carcasses from that tall stump. Word in town is that Floyd shot a lot of deer.

Thirty feet off the southwest corner of my house is a black walnut tree with a bifurcated trunk that climbs to a series of oddly twisted branches that don't seem quite natural. When it becomes bare in the winter it will remind me of the gnarly, ornery apple-throwing trees in *The Wizard of Oz*. But even in summer, sheathed in a cool, shady mass of mint-leaf-shaped foliage, the tree seems to be working too hard for a living.

"I've got a black walnut tree at home that would put that tree to shame," my father had told Reiger the Realtor when we first saw the house. He wasn't bragging as much as it sounds. The plush green carpet that is his backyard is ornamented by a nearly perfectly shaped black walnut, an Arbor Day poster child of a tree. It began life as a nut my father pocketed at a sun-bleached highway rest stop just inside the Texas border, where we'd taken a break on the last of our four-day journey to my start at college. The significance of his returning halfway across the country to a childless house, putting that nut into the ground, and nurturing it into a strong, supple tree was lost on me for many years. By the time I actually graduated from college, ten years later, that tree certainly had a firmer foothold in life than I did. Somehow, it seemed more prosperous. If it's possible to resent a tree, I did.

My parents often sit under that tree on summer evenings, and one of them reminds me an average of three visits out of every five that the nut came from Texas on the college trip. "I know," I remind them back. My father has spent a lot of time and energy trying to squirrel-proof the thing, but he is continually outwitted in ways that seem cartoonish. One moment he has finished wrapping the trunk with corrugated metal that will thwart any foothold by squirrel claws, when behind his back a team of the leaping rodents have started swinging onto branches from the clothesline. My mother enjoys the shade, but she whispers to me privately, "He's obsessed with that tree. It's *sad* to be obsessed by a black walnut tree."

On that first day of yard work, my green pants turn dark with perspiration. My arms are scratched bloody by thorns in the weed-whacker-resistant sumac, which must be cut and yanked by hand. We pile up a thick barricade of felled weeds, some with stalks as thick as my wrist. As we progress, my half-moon of property begins to look like a miniature Pas-schendael, a scarred wasteland of tiny stumps and craters, and it does seem that my war against weeds will be fought World War I style: no decisive victories, just a slight shifting of front lines, dirty battles of attrition. We sit on a log as the sunlight turns golden in the late afternoon. "Tough day today," my father says, rubbing his legs. Then he drives the hour home.

I virtually crawl into the house and fall onto my hard homemade bed and lie there prostrate and nearly comatose with fatigue. How do people work this hard every day? I think about the primping iron pumpers at my city health club and how they strutted around the air-conditioned, music-filled, carpeted room like peacocks. I wish I could tell them, *Try working a day with my old man once. See how you strut.*

The next morning is a first for me. I have an alcohol-free hangover. I am nauseated and achy simply from too much physical work. My father shows up—on time—and hefts a five-gallon plastic bucket from the trunk of his car. It is filled with bright green bulbs nearly the size of baseballs. They are nuts from his beloved black walnut tree. He has decided that we will spread them through my property and see if any take.

"You wanna pitch some?" he asks.

For seven years of my life I had heard that question so many times on summer nights that it resides in a place in my soul, the aural equivalent of the scent of cut grass, the spark of a hundred familiar fires of memory. We pitched some, my father and me. From May through September, we were tied by the orbital force of baseballs flying, held together at a distance of forty-six feet and six inches by the magnetism and gravity of devotion and practice. He was devoted; I practiced.

I feel slightly embarrassed trying to write about this. I've always had the cynic's sneer about rhapsodic tales of fathers and sons playing catch, and there seems to be no way to tell another one without scoring a movie scene in which the camera shot gets all gauzy and the soundtrack swells with the moan of cellos and the soaring, wide-open harmonies of French horns. It didn't seem like that when we were doing it. It was just what we did after dinner—*You wanna pitch some?*—another one of my father's improvement projects.

Of course, my father believed that anything was improved by the addition of concrete. In the driveway, he built a wood frame, a rectangle three inches deep and eight inches long that he filled with concrete to make a pitcher's rubber. He consulted the official rule book of Little League Baseball and followed the specs to the inch. Around the concrete block, he formed a mound using red clay that he had found somewhere, because red clay was what they used in major league baseball stadiums. Forty-six feet and six inches away—regulation distance—was a flagstone parking pad, onto which he painted a regulation-size home plate, pure white. Six feet behind that, he sunk two pipes into the ground on either side of the driveway, and then constructed a portable net of wire mesh that we could slide into those pipes. This was a backstop so that we wouldn't spend half the evening chasing passed balls.

And then we would go to work. This was not a casual game of catch in the backyard. It was training, and there was an obsessive nature to it that now strikes me as a little weird. As rigorous as we were, though, I never felt that I was being pushed into being a surrogate for my father's frustrated dreams of athletic prowess. I still don't. He liked to catch. And he wanted me to be able to pitch. I wanted the same thing. Sometimes as soon as dinner was over we'd be out there, my father still wearing his work clothes to save time, squatting behind the painted plate on a little plastic baby's chair to save his knees.

This started when I was eight. Although it would be several years before I became interested in music, in hindsight I think there was something about the mindless repetition and rhythm of the pitcher's motion, the setting, winding, twisting, throwing—the percussive pop as the ball hit the mitt—that appealed to whatever musical nature I had. Later, when I took up the trumpet, my parents sometimes had to plead with me to *stop* practicing.

If I hit the mitt exactly where my father had held the target, he would hold it there a few beats for effect, letting the echo of the drum shot die. *"That's* it," he'd say, and peg it back. I was not big and I was not strong. Talent would take me nowhere. I became the city's youngest junk pitcher, with a repertoire of overhand and sidearm and submarine deliveries and a sharp-breaking curveball that I shouldn't have been twisting my arm on at that age. But I became the all-star pitcher in my league. When it was time for the playoff games, my father didn't come. He said he had to work, but I think he was too nervous to attend.

Even today, when I find myself alone in my kitchen waiting for a pot of water to boil, I will set and slide into one of those pitching motions, throwing an invisible curveball through the window. I think when I no longer do this, I will be officially old. And I'll bet my father may have felt the same way back then.

Not long ago, I hunted down a well-known poem by Donald Hall. "Baseball is fathers and sons playing catch," he wrote. "Lazy and murderous, wild and controlled, the profound archaic song of birth, growth, age and death. This diamond discloses what we are." The title of the work almost says more than the poem itself. It is called "My Son, My Executioner."

Now I fire one of the green balls into the scrubby sumac woods behind my walnut tree. "Yeowwww," I yell. "There goes that arm." Tully is tossing them over into a bare spot to the south, where the previous owners had begun clearing for a horse corral and left a big dead tree in the middle of a scarred patch of caked dirt. I throw a dozen more nuts and stop. "I think my pitching days are over."

A few years ago at Christmas dinner at my sister's house, my father had gone on and on to visitors about what a pitcher I was and how he had built me this little field of dreams in the driveway. (It was more the bullpen for a field of dreams.) Tully got more animated as he talked, and he was clearly enjoying the memory, but it got a little windy. "Yeah," I finally said when I had heard enough, "maybe it would have been better if you'd built me a little concert hall to play my trumpet in." It got a laugh at the table. What a jerk I can be.

. . .

It was during these early weeks of work, after my father drove home and I slipped into the house in the late afternoon in desperate need of a nap, when I fully realized that my country retreat was about fifty feet from a state highway—a noisy state highway. One day I was complaining about this to the man I was renting my city apartment from, a psychologist who twenty-five years ago bought more than a hundred acres across the river in Pennsylvania. His professional opinion was that if you can't see the source of sound, you don't hear it as well. I pondered this for a few days and then decided that we needed to plant a row of hemlock trees out front—an eighty-five-foot row.

"Fine," my father said. "Plant them in a trench. Make it about a foot wide and a foot deep." He let me help him stretch and stake a guide line parallel to the road. It wasn't as close to the highway as I wanted it to be, but Tully, in his typical way, imagined the worst: that the state's highway department would come and make me tear the trees out if they were too close.

He handed me one long-handled pointed shovel and a pick that had been used so much that the points were as smooth and round as the head of a catfish. He nodded toward the length of yellow nylon string we'd stretched and said, "Go ahead. Dig a ditch." Then he went home, and stayed home.

I dug. For two days I dug. At first, that piece of string seemed Euclidian—a line that stretched to infinity. But after I'd sliced the topsoil off with the shovel, I entered an Einsteinian world where time and space seemed relative—relative to the number of buried rocks that seemed to increase exponentially as I burrowed deeper into the soil. There were minutes that seemed like hours as I swung the heavy pick.

I've read the passage in *Anna Karenina* in which Levin sheds his aristocratic robes and works with the peasants, realizing the joy of honest hard, hard labor. I tried, I really tried to make this experience ennobling and meaningful, thinking of it variously as a Zen exercise in selflessness, a Protestant project in self-improvement, a Catholic rite of penance. But nothing took me too far from the fact, the soggy painful fact, that I was digging a hole, and it was hard as hell. Tolstoy was full of it.

But I finished. I leaned on the pick and surveyed the results. Six blisters, eight piles of stones of various sizes, a throbbing lower back, and a long, skinny gash in the ground. I hobbled across the road to Floyd's property and started pulling little hemlocks out of the hillside. Floyd had given me permission.

I was leaning on that pick again when my father came back to help me plant—he's an accomplished vegetable gardener. Santino came that day, too.

They climbed up the slope from the driveway and stood, as men stand by the hundreds across America each day on every road project in every state, staring intently into a hole.

"Do you see the ditch John dug?" Tully asked his brother. "It's a good trench—nice and straight."

"Yeah," my uncle said. "That's straight."

"You know," my father continued, "his grandfather dug tunnels."

"Yeah," said Santino. "And his other grandfather was always working in dirt."

Tully chuckled at this. "His other grandfather," he said, "worked in shit all his life." They both laughed at that, and looked at the hole some more. I leaned on the pick some more.

Finally, my father concluded: "It must be in his blood."

Cue the cellos and the French horns. How proud he seemed. How proud the boy I was would be of the man I've become. At last, we have determined that I am The Natural in one pursuit. Digging ditches.

9.

Woodchucks
and Squirrels

November arrives, and we have made plans, lots of plans, but little progress. My red oak is outdoing itself, blazing crimson in the backyard. The black walnut's leaves have tinted slightly, and the hard green-shelled nuts are dropping. Out front by the road, the thin little hemlocks stand limp and tentative in a row, typical fresh recruits, swaying in the cool fall breeze. Tully and I are twiddling our thumbs.

We're waiting for help. We've decided to tear apart the house from the top down. I realize it would be stupid not to keep things simple. This house is solid, and its virtue lies in its simplicity and plainness. The best thing to do is bring it up to date—new plumbing, new wiring, new windows, a new roof—and make it a home that will stand sturdy for another half a century. The only major structural addition will be a large dormer cut into the rear side of the second floor to add a bathroom upstairs and a closet for each of the two bedrooms.

That doesn't sound like too difficult a job to me. The roof shingles on the west side have to be stripped off. Next, nine rafters will be cut out of the center of the main roof. Then the dormer—essentially a miniature house, twelve feet wide by eight feet deep—has to be built inside that hole, with its own little roof turned at a right angle to the main roof. When that's done, the main roof and the dormer roof have to be newly shingled. I have drawn the plans on a new pad of grid paper, feeling a little twinge of déjà vu from the blueprint-filled days of my youth. Then I relearn one of those disheartening lessons of youth. Daddy does not know everything.

"I can't do this," Tully tells me one day.

"Why not?"

"What the hell do you think I am? I don't have scaffolding. I don't have the tools I need to cut open that roof. I'm not a roofer. We gotta get someone in to do that dormer. Just have him do the roof and build the shell. The inside we can do ourselves."

"This is supposed to be a do-it-yourself project."

"This is a big job," Tully says. "If you were in Scranton, maybe we could do it ourselves. I could borrow the scaffold and all that stuff. I could get some help. But I can't ask guys to drive all the way out here."

"This is like framing a small shed," I tell him. "It's just cutting open the roof—"

"You don't know what you're talkin' about," he interrupts. "It's a big job. A big job. You gotta know what you're doin'. You gotta have the right tools. You can't read about this in a book."

Ouch. He has noticed the pile of how-to books accumulating next to my futon bed. The books I'm reading now all have the same riveting plot—do it yourself.

We stare at the Weather Channel for a few minutes, each of us stewing. High pressure is building in the Northwest. "All right," I finally say. "I'll start asking around about contractors. I wasn't expecting this. I'm not sure if my budget will cover a lot of outside work."

"Don't worry about the money," he says. "I can give you money. I might as well give it to you now instead of waiting till I die."

Meeting with local contractors becomes an odd introduction to my new neighbors. Reiger the Realtor sends over a cousin who is chatty and scattered and doesn't listen to a word I say. But he invites me to some kind of barbecue he's throwing, and a few days later leaves a bid for a project that bears little resemblance to what I want done.

A friendly guy from a small construction company in Pennsylvania drives across the river to visit and estimate the job. My father does all the talking, but the contractor knows it's my house and he asks me to help him measure the dimensions. We're stretching a long, contractor-grade tape down the length of my foundation, and my father says to him, "You're going to trust *his* measurement?" The contractor looks at Tully, looks and me, and takes a diplomatic chance. "Yeah," he says. "It doesn't have to be perfect."

Two young guys who seem to be hauling a lot of attitude with them in their pickup truck come by. "We usually only do historical renovations," the one in charge tells me. "Restoring barns and that kind of thing." It turns out he has married into the local elite, the supermarket magnates of the river valley. He brings back a bid that is so outrageously high that when my father sees it he says, "Call him and ask him, 'What the hell are you gonna put on that roof, gold leaf?' "

I've learned by now that a high bid often means the contractor is simply not interested in getting the job. But this bid insults even my limited intelligence of construction matters. I'm tempted to try to gaslight him, call and say, "Gosh, Steve, this is the best price we got. You must be losing money on this, but, hey, that's your business. When can you start?"

Another guy shows up in full camouflage and quotes us a decent price, but warns that he doesn't want this work to interfere with his hunting.

Then one morning the phone rings early—really early— and the voice on the other end of the line forces me to hold the receiver two inches from my ear. "Hey, this is Lou Meckle from over the hill. I heard you're tryin' to reach me."

"Yeah, Lou," I say, trying to see the clock. It's too dark. Lou Meckle is highly thought of in the area, but reputed to be busier than a man should be. Sleep-addled, I try to explain the job to him. "Can you come over and look at it and give me an estimate?"

"Well," he says, "I might could make it over there today.

But it's gotta be in the afternoon. Gotta dig a grave this mornin'."

"Whenever you can, Lou. I'll be here."

Since it's nearly seven, I call my father. By this time of day, he has committed to memory the five-day weather forecasts for all fifty states. We had planned to take the day off. We've done just about every odd job imaginable by now and are basically inventing busy work. I've become the Cal Ripken of the local hardware store, making a daily appearance and a small contribution. "Ah, I need a two-inch stopper for a slop sink . . . ah, seven three-inch bolts . . . ah, and some window putty." The owner—a young man named John Grund, who has the sad eyes of a hound and a droopy mustache—is helpful and friendly, despite the fact that he is often forced to ring up a sale that requires me to give him only change from my pocket. He amuses himself by putting wry messages on the mobile sign in his parking lot, where he should be advertising sale prices on plumbing supplies. Instead, it often features some whimsical phrase like his hunting season slogan: "Support shoot and release." When I find myself spending a lot of each day thinking of clever suggestions for John's sign, I know we really need to find a contractor and get started.

"Lou Meckle said he'd be over today," I tell my father.

"I'll be up," he says.

It takes some doing to make my father look like a city slicker, but Lou Meckle pulls it off. He drives up in an elaborately shelled black pickup truck that looks as if the painted logo on it should read "Darth Vader, Contractor." The man who emerges from the cab looks as if he might have wandered off the set of *Hee Haw*—or as if he might have *built* the set of *Hee Haw*. He is squat and thick as a tree trunk, decked out in layers of faded flannel and dirty brown Carhartt overalls. He approaches us a little shyly and sticks out a big hand. Shaking hands with Lou Meckle is like trying to get a grip on a huge, callused ham.

He and Tully are instantly buddies, work buddies. They talk of the carpenters union and various jobs they've done over the years, before Lou went into business for himself. Maybe they were on some project together? My father had come into this area a few times, to work on new buildings at the summer Borscht Belt resorts a half hour east. At the time, it was a two-hour drive each way from Scranton.

"In those days, we'd go anywhere for work," Tully says. "Not like the kids today." The two older men nod and grunt and look over at me. Am I supposed to defend myself? Defend Youth itself? *Hey*, I could say, *I've gone all the way to Paris for work*. But I don't want to take the chance that Lou Meckle would take his big hard ham of a fist and swat me across the driveway, after which my father, trying to do the right thing for his son, would walk over and kick me.

In the end, they can't come up with any job they've worked together, though obviously they are two guys with a lot in common. Finally, Lou breaks the small talk with, "Well, let's take a look at 'er."

We spend fifteen minutes in the backyard, pointing up at the roof and making sure that Lou sees the same dormer in his mind that I see in mine. Then we clomp into the house and up the stairs. Lou hits the landing, turns into the smaller bedroom, and gazes at the vault of varnished knotty pine. "So," he says, "we're not gonna touch this, are we?"

"He wants to tear it out," Tully tells Lou with that special tone parents use to talk about the mistakes of their headstrong children who just won't listen. It has been a continuing tug of war of taste as I've tried to convince Tully that the knotty pine has to go. Now he has an ally to help him pull against me. "Look at that," my father says. "You can't get boards like that nowadays—you'd pay a fortune."

Lou makes an appreciative grunt.

"It's coming out," I say.

Lou senses a situation he'd rather not enter and gives another, more noncommittal grunt. Then we move through the specifications for cutting open the roof and supporting the new walls.

"Looks like you had some squirrels up here," Lou says.

"Oh, you wouldn't believe it," my father tells him.

After Lou Meckel leaves, my father tells me, "He's your guy."

It turns out he is. Lou's bid is not the lowest, but reasonable—a bargain compared with the barn restorers.

"Okay, Lou," I tell him on the phone. "We're on. You want to bring over a contract?" Everything I've read in my stack of books tells me to get a very specific contract.

"Nah," he says. "I don't see no need for that."

It is one of those times where I have to decide whether to trust what I've read in a book or to go with my instincts. Lou Meckle seems like the kind of guy you could trust with the secret code to your checking account. I decide in a moment that his word is as good as a contract. "When can you start?" I ask Lou. "We'd really like to get this thing going."

"We got us a few things to finish first. Imagine it shouldn't be more'n a week or so. I'll keep in touch."

The next time a simple hard-handed man dressed in flannel tells me something with the plain homeliness of Abe Lincoln, I will treat him as if he's wearing a cheap plaid suit and selling band instruments that you can learn to play using the Think System.

It turns out the Meckle method of keeping in touch is having his wife or daughter tell you he's out on a job and then not calling back.

Three weeks go by. "You hear from Lou?" my father asks.

"No."

"Did you call him?"

"*Yes*, I called him."

"Call him again."

"I've called him twice. I'm paying him. *He* should call back."

"You gotta get over that."

We spend our time shopping, visiting warehouses for things like bathroom fixtures and electrical goods, becoming habitués of Scranton's home-supply stores. My father is calling in every chit he's ever received, and in most of the places we go, we immediately get the contractor's discount price. The trouble is, over weeks of shopping, the only object we can actually agree on is a little wheelbarrow that's on sale at Home Depot, and I buy it retail. One day we're using it to spread new gravel around my driveway when Floyd Campfield stops for a visit.

He rolls up to the house behind the wheel of a Ford farm tractor whose pistons fire with the sound of four guys in some sort of sledgehammer contest. Floyd jumps off the fanny-shaped tractor seat and comes over to introduce himself. To me, he is a legend come to life. This is what I have heard about Floyd: He grew up in the town, went into the army, came back to build this house, worked in the town lumberyard for a while, became a state policeman, shot a lot of deer, harvested the Delaware River for freshwater eels, smoked those eels in a shed on what is now my property, and begat four children, the eldest of whom is the other local legend I'm hoping to meet—Floyd Junior, known as Lurch.

"I heard somebody finally bought this place," Floyd says. He is a tall guy who was probably once a beanpole, a very strong beanpole, but who has gotten a little paunchy in retirement. He strides around back. "You might not believe me," he says, "but I built this place for five thousand dollars."

"That's what I paid," I tell him.

"That's not what I heard."

I keep forgetting that I am now living in a small town.

Floyd gives us the brief history of the place—whom he sold it to and who bought it from them, and who came in after that. "It's the last people who let this place go to hell," he says. "They were young kids. They didn't want to work. They wanted to ride horses or something.

"I was over here in the basement once," he continues, "and the whole place was filled with empty soda bottles. You shoulda seen it. A lot of soda bottles. They were *soda drinkers*, those people." He says this—"soda drinkers"—as if he were saying "child molesters." Yet Floyd's whole diatribe is delivered with such a matter-of-fact, commonplace attitude that I wonder if the entire town of Narrowsburg doesn't think this way, if it wouldn't curl its collective lip and spit out this description of the worst habit that can overtake a person—*"soda drinkers."*

My father figures Floyd can lead us to the Holy Grail of the septic tank. The location of the tank has become a major topic of conversation and speculation for us, as has its condition and potential for failure at any moment. Mister Worst Case Scenario will not be denied his grim predictions.

Floyd can't remember exactly where he put the septic tank, though he seems to remember the detail on every nail he'd driven and the cost of each windowpane. He gets ready to climb back onto the tractor. "You oughta look up my son," he says. "He works for Roto-Rooter. He can find that tank for you. I'll tell him about it. His name's Lurch."

There are some books that I read all the time, in the same way people listen to certain records over and over again. Walker Percy's *The Moviegoer* is one of them, and in it is a scene where Binx Bolling, the moviegoer, establishes his standing in a Tulane fraternity house by picking the perfectly apt nickname—descriptive and sardonic at once—for one of the new brothers. Binx could not have come up with anything better than Lurch.

The initial indication that I would finally meet him, this man whose childhood bedroom I am now using as an office, was sonic. I was sitting at the bar of the Narrowsburg Inn, a 150-year-old roadhouse in the middle of town that is one of two bars I can patronize comfortably. Based on appearances and a little asking around, I concluded that the Inn was the place where I would be least likely to be injured in a brawl. I had discovered the bar early in my tenure in town and started hanging out there to watch Yankees games. Part of my transition to country life was giving up television. When I finally took over the house after closing, I was prepared to fire up that twelve-foot satellite dish in my backyard and start beaming in cooking shows from Pluto. But the previous owners had taken off with the transponder. Now, to watch anything, I had to drive to the Inn.

The night I met Lurch, there was a sputtering cacophony outside the Inn of a motorcycle whose muffler sounded as if it had been hooked up in reverse, so that it actually amplified the engine noise. Miss Mary, the bartender, gave a pained look toward the door. A couple of customers turned their heads that way, and someone said, "There's Lurch." My first feeling was that I should clear out while there was still time.

Too late. In walked Lurch. He's about six foot four, lean as his father must have been, as sinewy and as scary-looking a man as I have ever seen in real life. He was wearing what I've since learned is his usual outfit: motorcycle boots, jeans rubbed with so much oil and dirt that it is hard to tell where the material stops and where the oil begins, and a black t-shirt whose short sleeves had been ripped off at the armpits. His face was covered by a thick, wiry black beard, the beard of an Old Testament prophet. On his head was a shiny World War I German field officer's helmet with a spike sticking out of the top.

Lurch walked around behind me, shook hands with a couple of people, and settled three stools away, next to a big olive-skinned woman who'd been sitting for a while, chatting easily with other customers and Miss Mary. Lurch unhooked his helmet and had a beer placed before him without having to order. The Inn, I would learn, kept several cases of his favorite beer just for him. No one else ever ordered it. One thing was clear: Lurch was no damn soda drinker. He took a couple of gulps from the long-necked bottle and sat, his leg pumping with the nervous piston motion of a teenager trapped in a late-spring classroom. Then he jumped up to play the pinball machine. I decided to stay for another drink or so and maybe get acquainted.

About an hour passed, and I had made no move. Lurch scared me. Finally, probably after sensing that I'd been observing her and her husband the whole time, Lurch's wife, Anna Campfield, turned to me and said, "Excuse me, but who the hell are you?"

That's how I was drawn into the land of Lurch. I still can't say we're friends, exactly—he never would tell me where my septic tank is located—but he has become for me the exemplar of the Woodchuck. It is what the outsiders, the city people with weekend houses, call the locals to put them down; it is what the locals call themselves to feel superior to the out-of-towners.

When my psychologist landlord from the city heard that I was giving up my apartment in Manhattan, he asked me, "You really think you're ready to become a Woodchuck?"

Using Lurch as the model, I considered. You spend the day working at your plumbing job. Then you might tear the engine out of your truck and replace it, or work on the deck addition to your house, or chop the five cords of lumber you're planning to use to heat the house through the winter, or shoot a deer. Then you go out for a couple of cocktails.

Everyone's favorite story about Lurch comes from the

night he and his younger brother were thrown out of another bar for being a little too rowdy during a pool game. The Campfield boys went home, got their chainsaws, and went back to the bar, threatening to saw the pool table in half.

At some point on any given evening, Lurch might be stomping around the dance floor of the Inn, or shooting the shit with his buddies from the local motorcycle gang, or, if he gets really drunk, hugging many of the people at the bar (he knows just about everybody in town) and even affectionately licking a few, his bristly beard scratching their cheeks as they try to push him away—*"Okay, Lurch, that's enough now, c'mon."* It's not unusual for Lurch to make it through last call at the Inn. God only knows what happens next. I have seen Anna Campfield, with an audience, reach under the bar to grab Lurch's oil-stained crotch and announce, "You think I married him for his brains?" In any case, there's a good chance he'll be out the next morning by six A.M. to plow driveways before going to work.

I thought about Lurch's life and about my life. No, I was not quite ready to be a Woodchuck.

The morning after I meet Anna and Lurch, I stumble through the early part of the day in a painful daze.

"What the hell's the matter with you?" my father asks.

"I was out kind of late last night at the Inn."

"This shit's gotta stop. If you wanna work."

We're getting the upstairs ready for the alleged arrival of Lou Meckle. That means tearing down the walls and the ceilings. Every piece of Sheetrock that comes down reveals another clue to the extent to which this house has become a Club Med for squirrels.

"Sons-of-bitchin' squirrels," my father shouts as we yank down a piece of plasterboard and a rain of squirrel-dung pellets falls onto his head and shoulders. "I can't believe it. They ruined this place."

The second floor of my house has a roofline like you see in a converted attic. Knee walls come up four feet from the floors, then the ceiling runs up at a diagonal to seven feet, and then there's a regular ceiling parallel to the floor running in a six-foot-wide band in the center. We will remove about fifteen hundred square feet of old Sheetrock as we gut the upstairs. Barely six inches of that has not been infiltrated by rodents.

The squirrels have left nuts, pieces of nuts, marbles, coins, pine cones, kids' toys, several small skeletons of their departed brethren, and so much rice-kernel-sized dung that I could probably use it to heat the house through the winter, except I don't have a fireplace. After the Sheetrock is down, I start ripping the old insulation from where it is stapled to the rafters and the outside walls. The paper backing says, "New! Dow Corning, Two-Inch Fiberglass." It was probably the latest in heat-loss prevention in Floyd's day. But the squirrels have done something with the pink fiberglass over the years. Eaten it? Played with it? Appropriated it to cozy up their nests? Mostly, I roll up only old parchment-like paper filled with little lumps of squirrel shit.

"Bastard squirrels," my father says. He is developing a repertoire of squirrel epithets.

Uncle Santino, taking a cue from his older brother, settles on calling them "sons-of-bitchin' squirrels" and generally sticks to that, muttering it constantly as he mans a big warehouse broom that he has brought up with him. Uncle Santino has a museum-quality broom collection and has begun to acquire and curate one for me. We sweep and gather. Pile upon pile of dung goes into trash bags. Most of it is petrified pellets, but there are places in the outside walls where it has settled and baked over the years into square lumps the size of bricks. I wear a pair of gloves that are soon stained black as we work, and I remember Reiger the Realtor telling me, "They had a little problem with some squirrels up in the second floor." Caveat emptor. *A little problem!* Should I sue? Should I light a brick of squirrel dung on Reiger's front porch, ring the doorbell, and run away?

We have become amateur squirrel behaviorists. We sit at lunch downstairs and theorize about their habits.

How do you think they got in?

Did they live here all the time, or just in winter?

What do you think they did with the insulation?

How could they produce so much shit?

Tully outlines his plan to squirrel-proof the place. Like most of my father's plans, it involves doing something physically onerous and using materials that he happens to have lying around his house. Basically, anything that comes into my father's possession never leaves the house. He has washed and saved every plastic container of deli food he has ever purchased, and they are stacked in tall cylinders that have overgrown the kitchen cupboards and have started filling the basement. If we nailed them together, we could build the new dormer with plastic deli containers.

For squirrels, he wants to use wire lath left over from his days in construction. Wire lath is a diamond-shaped mesh of

stainless steel that my father attached to walls and ceilings so
that wet plaster would have something to grab on to. It is as
sharp as razors and very difficult to work with. I remember
that his hands were always scarred with a random scattering
of small cuts, as if he'd been fighting with cats all day. Working with wire lath, he was never able to wear a wedding ring,
for fear that it would catch on the lath as he worked quickly
and tear off his finger. If I had wrestled with this stuff every
day for thirty years, I would never want to see it again, but
my father feels comfortable with the lath. His plan calls for
us to cut pieces of this stuff to fit into every opening we can
find in the walls between the first floor and the second, and
then nail it over the openings. "That's the only way they can
be gettin' in," my father speculates.

A few days later, I am crawling on my belly into the tight
triangular space where the bottom edge of the roof rests on
the plate of the first-floor walls. My father really wants to do
this, I can see, but I've taken the job away from him. It
doesn't seem like a project for a man who has turned seventy-
four. And I don't even want to mention that I don't think
both he and his belly will fit into the space. With my face
scraping the floorboards, I stretch into the corner and try to
get a folding wood ruler out of my pocket and into a spot
that's clearly a squirrel tunnel. Looking down the length of
the house, I can see that there are twenty-eight of these
holes—on each side. Another fun day of work.

I finally manage to unfold the ruler and get my arm
around to take the measurement, and I see that Tully has
handed me a ruler whose front end is broken off, so that I'll
have to measure in reverse, counting down from twelve feet.

"This is the wrong end of the ruler," I call back to where he's standing, just behind the bare studs of the knee wall.

"Don't you know how to take a measurement from the wrong end of a ruler?" he asks.

"I know how to subtract," I say.

"All you gotta do is count the numbers backwards and take the lower number from the higher number," he says.

"That's what I just said," I call back. "I know how to subtract."

"I had kids workin' with me who couldn't figure that out."

"I went to college."

"Hey, goin' to college doesn't make you smart."

That settled, he cuts the wire lath to the measurements I call out and then passes it to me, and I try to hammer the small sharp sheet into place. My hammer skills are low even in open spaces. Here, it's like trying to play Whack-a-Mole inside a coffin. I can't lift the hammer head more than two or three inches, which makes me hit the nails from an angle. With each anemic blow, nails disappear down into the squirrel tunnel, or fly back into my face, or skitter across the floor. One lands at my father's feet, and he says with a weary voice, "You want me to crawl in there and do that?"

"I don't think you'll fit in here," I tell him.

"The hell I won't." In the end, he puts in most of the squirrel barriers himself.

Over the next few days, the weather turns cold and we're down to the bare rafters in half of the upstairs. Replacement insulation is stacked around the rooms, shrink-wrapped in plastic. The paper-lined rolls for the walls are round and plump and look like bales of hay. The flat, fluffy sheets for the ceiling (called "batts") are long and wide; stacked atop one another, the packages are as inviting as a chaise lounge. What little original insulation was left is all gone now. While we're working, our conversations come in short bursts of steam, like misty thought bubbles. Tully generally voices just one thought: "I wish the hell Lou would get here."

Later that week, again stuck with nothing to do, the baseball season over, I begin a self-improvement project—reading Shakespeare's plays. In *Hamlet* I find a short stanza that must be among history's most elegant couplets dedicated to the subject of house insulation.

Imperious Caesar, dead and turned to clay
Might stop a hole to keep the wind away
O, that that earth, which kept the world in awe,
Should patch a wall to expel the winter's flaw!

I receive some information in the mail from an insulation manufacturer. One brochure has a question on its cover: "What's Insulation Got to Do with Regret, Breathing, and Money?" All of a sudden, there seem to be worlds of meaning behind what I stuff into my walls. A decision that I considered simple becomes loaded with portent.

When next I see the King of the Woodchucks, Lurch actually shakes my hand at the bar of the Inn. I am becoming a regular. That night I am thinking of squirrels and Shakespeare and insulation, and I have had three glasses of Scotch in a vain attempt to expel the oncoming winter's flaw. On a pad I write:

If I'm to become the king of batts
I cannot blame the common rat.
For though I can't say boy or girl
I know the culprit is a squirrel

Oh, I wish the hell Lou Meckle would get here.

10.

There Might Be
a Name for It

In the dull gray light of dawn, I reach in a sleepy panic for the ringing phone.

"Hey, this is Lou Meckle. Expect you'll be seein' us over there first thing Wednesday mornin'."

Hallelujah, Lou.

Wednesday arrives, the day before Thanksgiving. The morning sky is a thick, roiling blanket of slate-gray clouds. A dandruffy sprinkle of snow is whorled by a hard northwest wind. At ten minutes to seven, a small gray pickup truck pulls into my driveway and sits there; whoever is behind the wheel stays inside. I sit up on the futon and look out and see through the truck's rear window a man drinking coffee as if he were performing a Balinese shadow puppet play.

A little after seven, Lou Meckle arrives driving an ancient black Ford cabin truck with a homemade wooden bed filled with iron-pipe scaffolding. Lou's choice of transportation gives him an image much more rakish than his real self. This vehicle looks as if it could have been used to smuggle liquor from Canada during Prohibition. He negotiates the truck past my huge satellite dish, between the black walnut tree and the red oak, throws it with a clunk into reverse, and backs toward the rear of the house. The man in the Japanese pickup jumps out. Another young guy comes out of the passenger side of the Ford. For the first time in my life, I have a crew.

But it is quickly clear that I am hardly in charge. The crew—Lou Meckle, his son Lou Junior, and their hired man Al—are not accustomed to having a well-meaning incompetent running around trying to help. They move wordlessly through what seems to me a kind of choreography, erecting the scaffolding, tier upon tier, swinging the Lego-like metal bars in one-handed hook shots over their shoulders. When this structure of pipes is completed, my crew will use it as their gangplank to tear the shingles from my roof and cut a big hole in the house where the dormer will be inserted.

Helping as best I can, I try to steady a piece of pipe, but I have to ask which end goes up. They look at me as if someone has entered their dance routine wearing ski boots, all the while politely trying not to make it obvious that I am really in the way and a huge pain in the ass. Eventually, I figure it out myself, and retreat inside the house to make some coffee.

My father arrives a few minutes past nine. He is happy this morning and smiles in a way that shows most of his new teeth. A whole new set was implanted just before he retired from his city job, which carried what he still refers to as a "Cadillac health plan." The teeth cost nearly as much as he ever made in a year. Tully, it turns out, was a tooth grinder; he'd simply worn out his original set, a little bit every night. He's probably started on the new ones.

For weeks, he's been grumpy and out of sorts. After a Scranton shopping trip, I had stopped to chat with one of his neighbors. "Your father's really dying to get his hands on that house," said Pat Trunzo, the retired cop down the road. "He can't wait."

"Hey, Louuuuuu," Tully shouts up into the scaffolding. "How ya doin'? You need any help?"

"We're fine here, John."

Lou Meckle is a no-nonsense worker who doesn't waste time talking. By the time I have finished my second cup of coffee, the scaffolding is up and he knocks on my door. Over his shoulder is a sawhorse made of two-by-six lumber that is so weathered the wood looks prehistoric. The scattered scars of saw cuts form patterns that would fascinate and perplex a team of archaeologists. Hunched under the weight of the sawhorse, the squat Lou Meckle himself seems some kind of missing link who has been gussied up in flannels and stiff work clothes. I look at the label on his overalls and dub him Carhartt Man.

"You want some coffee, Lou?" I ask as he navigates through the doorway.

"Had my coffee," he says, and keeps moving toward the stairs.

"You wouldn't want his coffee anyway," my father tells Lou. "It tastes lousy. I don't know how anybody can drink it."

My coffee is said to be the best arabica beans available from the prime suppliers of the growing countries of Central and South America, roasted under exacting conditions in the Pacific Northwest and then vacuum sealed and air shipped by Federal Express to me. I spend more time and money on my coffee than I do on my wardrobe. Tully thinks it's another of my yuppie affectations—like buying new shoes when the old ones could be resoled, or spending money at a restaurant when you could make perfectly good food at home.

Within thirty minutes, Lou has erected a workbench upstairs and we begin to hear a muffled bowling-alley sound as Lou Junior and Al climb onto the roof and start stripping it of shingles.

"John," Lou calls down from the second floor, "I need you up here to be my architect."

He gets both Johns. But Lou makes it clear that since I am the guy who will write the check, I am the guy he will listen to. My father takes a half step back, looking a little hurt and insulted.

Lou crawls behind the knee wall with a new two-by-four. He places it on the floor, at a right angle to the rear wall. "Okay, this'll be the wall of the dormer on this side," he says. The board is set just inches from a pipe that comes up from the kitchen sink, the vent pipe that allows air to enter through the roof and into the plumbing loop. The main drainpipe in a house works like a big straw with a lot of other small straws feeding into it. If the various kitchen and bathroom drains didn't have this source of ventilation, it would be as if someone were holding a finger over the top of the straw. The water simply would not drain out.

"Can we get that pipe inside the dormer?" my father asks. "We should connect it to the main stack."

"That'd be all right," Lou says. "But I'm not a plumber."

He hands me a tape measure and says to go over and find twelve feet from the new board to mark where the south wall will be.

"You're going to trust his measurement?" my father asks. Again.

It's my turn to be hurt and insulted. "You want to do it?" I ask.

"No, go ahead."

In only a few minutes we have laid out a three-dimensional wooden diagram for the dormer. I still can't understand why we're not doing this job ourselves. Then Lou goes out on the scaffolding to join Lou Junior and Al, who are stripping the roof of its shingles. The roof is pitched steeply, ten inches of drop for every foot of horizontal run. Watching these experienced guys gingerly navigate across the angled face of it, I begin to appreciate why my father backed off this job. The work they do is quick and dirty. My backyard, which so much labor went into making weed free, is soon covered with pieces of faded green shingles. It looks like someone has smashed a big asphalt cookie.

Dusk comes early, and the Meckle team stops.

"We'll be seein' ya on Saturday, I suppose," Lou tells me as he's leaving. "Tomorrow's Thanksgivin', and Friday's first day a' deer season. I always try to get that one day in."

I'm so happy they've made even a bit of progress that I wouldn't try to argue, even though Lou originally promised that once he started he'd be in and out within a week.

On Saturday, Lou moves back inside, and I really start to understand my father's reluctance in taking on this job. Hefting a reciprocating saw, a tool that looks like the head of a particularly gruesome animatronic swordfish, Lou rips open a big hole in the roof. The work is heavy and crude, yet it must be executed precisely enough that a perfectly square new box can be fitted inside the opening.

My father is everywhere. He seems to be embarrassed that he's had to punt on this job, and he is making up for it by being absurdly helpful. As soon as Lou has created a pile of sawdust, Tully is on it with a broom. "I don't know about you, Lou," he says, "but I always like to keep the work area clean."

"That's fine, John."

Lou, I sense, would just as soon wade knee-deep in sawdust as talk while he's trying to work.

At lunchtime, my father and I sit at the plastic patio table in my dining room, or at least what will eventually be the dining room. It is now a room filled with whatever won't fit somewhere else. Tully is slurping a thick soup I've made from butternut squash, cream, chicken broth, and a little bit of white port wine. The recipe comes from *Gourmet* magazine. "What the hell kind of soup is this?" he asked when he saw me crumbling goat cheese on top of it. "What's that?"

"It's goat cheese," I told him.

"Goat cheese. Jesus."

Now he can't get enough. He is a single-minded eater; like a prisoner, he stares into his bowl, his spoon moving relentlessly until the bowl is clean. I hear the scraping sound of metal on ceramic. After his second serving, Tully puts the spoon down and admits, "That was pretty good."

We're upstairs. Downstairs in my basement, Lou and his son and Al sit on stacked lumber in the cold, eating steamy, mushy stuff out of wide-mouth thermoses. I have peeked down the new stairs several times and tried to lure them up, but each time Lou refuses. It could be a standard nonfraternization rule he follows. It could be that we are driving him nuts, hanging around and watching him do his job.

The afternoon is a race to frame the dormer and at least get a tarp over it to close the hole against the weather. Through the day, the sky seems to get heavier, and as the weak light wanes further, the damp smell of snow permeates the air. The worst-case scenario is that I wake up on a Sunday with snowdrifts in my second floor, a situation my father has presented to me in vivid detail several times already, larding his dire predictions with technical phrases he has learned from the Weather Channel. "What *are* 'lake-effect storms'?" I finally ask him.

"We gonna get closed in today, Lou?" Tully keeps asking.

Lou grunts. "I'm movin' as fast as I can, John."

"You need any help, just let me know," Tully says. "You can put me on the payroll. I'm willing to work."

"Uh-huh."

I have tried to stay downstairs and out of the way most of the day. In midafternoon, I climb up into the second floor and see Lou swing a long two-by-six rafter around and almost knock my father's head off as he straightens from picking up another pile of sawdust.

"I gotta swing my boards, John," Lou snaps. "Ya just gotta keep outta my way so I can do that."

It is nearly heartbreaking to see the realization creep into my father's face like a blush. He is in the way, and now he knows it. He decides to leave early that afternoon.

Before he drives off, I tell him, "I'm going to go away for a couple days. I feel fine about giving Lou a key and letting him work on his own."

"Nah," Tully says. "I'll be up first thing Monday morning."

When I get back late on Monday afternoon, I find the entire crew upstairs. Lou Junior and Al are outside, placing beams for the ceiling of the dormer. Lou Meckle is inside, working with the new wood, cutting boards to fit. My father is hanging around, and I lure him downstairs.

"You shoulda been here earlier," he says. "You coulda seen how a water level works. Lou needed to get his level marks for the dormer beams, and I got my water level out and did it for them." Tully sounds like the nerdy guy at school who is pleased with himself because the cool kids have allowed him to help write their term papers.

A water level is a clear plastic hose. Since water always seeks its own level, if you fill the hose and hold one end to where the bubble on top marks a line—say, the top of a wall—the water on the other end of the hose will settle at exactly that same height. Using it, you can actually walk around the corner of a wall and accurately mark a standard height. These days, contractors use lasers to do this job, but my father would no sooner buy a laser than he would a graphite hammer. "The water level still works for me," he says.

"They didn't think they needed it," my father says, lowering his voice and gesturing upstairs to where Lou is working. "But I got it out, and now they have good marks to work with. That dormer'll be level."

We climb back up to the second floor. By now, the dormer is mostly framed, and sheets of plywood have been nailed around the walls. The sloped ceiling is still open, and the two rooms are flooded with light. The sky is a bright winter blue, and Lou Meckle has brought in a torpedo-shaped heater to fight the cold. It pumps out a moist, roaring wave of heat. I imagine my electric meter spinning out of control.

From the roof, Lou Junior shouts down measurements to his father, who is cutting the last of the rafters for the new dormer. The roofline of the new dormer runs at a right angle to the roofline of the house. The rafters of the dormer roof get progressively shorter as they get closer to the main roof. The saw cuts Lou must make here are compound; the boards fit in like puzzle pieces.

"That's powerful close," Lou Junior shouts as he passes a short just-cut dormer rafter back to his father. "But it's gotta come off another quarter inch."

Lou makes the correction freehand, maneuvering his big contractor-grade heavy-duty circular saw as easily as if he were cutting bread dough. He passes the clean new lumber back up through the hole in the roof.

"That's got her," his son shouts. I wonder if I will ever be able to work with Tully like this. He is so easily frustrated and I am so easily offended that the possibility seems remote. I move into the light near Lou and watch him make more saw cuts, angle upon angle.

Lou makes a series of particularly complicated passes over a board, the oddly shaped discard pieces dropping to the floor like children's blocks.

"Is there a name for that cut?" I ask.

Lou Meckle puts the saw down on his workbench. A puff of sawdust rises into the air, blown into visible movement by the steady blast of the torpedo heater. He looks at me.

"Well," he says, "there might be a name for it—if you don't know how to do it."

There might be a name for it, if you don't know how to do it.

Here I am, prepared to pay this guy about a thousand dollars for each day he and his two men show up to work on my house. This freckled, round little man who has proudly told me that his white-collar daughter has been all the way to Las Vegas, but little else about anything—this guy nonchalantly reduces the last fifteen years of my life to one sentence. That's what I've been doing all this time: naming stuff I don't know how to do. I have ridden with cowboys on a cattle drive, been splattered by warm Texas crude while a young oil man saw his fortune rise up in a gusher, sat sipping coffee with senators and governors, questioned CEOs as if I had a clue about what makes a business run. And then I've returned home and molded my mass of misapprehensions into a heap of words. I have presumed to size up the character of a man with no more than a lunch between us. How silly and useless I must seem to a guy like Lou Meckle. How silly I seem to myself. There might be a name for it.

· · ·

We definitely don't know how to do plumbing. Lou Meckle had recommended a local guy who gave me an estimate that was three times too high but who assumed he had the job since Lou had the job. The morning after I talked to him, his helper showed up with a load of pipes to start working. Tully turned him away at the door. Then I had to do the explaining to the boss over the telephone. He was one unhappy Woodchuck. Tully spent the night calling his contractor contacts and found someone who lived about fifteen miles away and who'd just started a plumbing business of his own. He comes in time to put that main plumbing stack through the roof of the new dormer just before the Meckle crew is ready to nail on the shingles. The other plumber dropped by in the morning and talked to Lou for a few minutes. I saw him pointing at me from inside his truck, but he never got out. There's snow and a little tension in the air this afternoon.

Bob, the new plumber, does his best to smooth the ruffled feathers on everyone. He is a man who has read the self-help canon, it seems, and taken it to heart. If you act cheery, you will be cheery. With Bob it works. And it spreads.

Bob is a tall man with a big, hooked nose and shaggy blond hair. Over the next months he will be at my house a score of times, and I cannot remember him ever wearing anything but the outfit he wears on that first day—black jeans, plaid flannel shirt, and down vest. He likes my coffee, and he likes to chat. After the main vent pipe is in place, he settles against the kitchen counter and tells me that he really has to get going to make a class early this evening at a college in Pennsylvania. After working in construction for twenty years, he's trying to get a degree in education. "After that,"

Bob says, "I'm thinkin' about divinity school. I'd really like to end up in some kind of pastoral work."

Trained as I am to name things I can't do, I tell Bob he should go with the religious theme for his new business. I look outside at his blank white van and picture a logo. "You should call yourself the Pope of Pipes," I tell him, "or something like that."

Now it's his turn to be insulted.

After the dormer is fully framed and sealed, Lou Meckle disappears from the job and the finish work falls to Lou Junior and Al. They work together with an easy banter. From out on the scaffolding, Al calls in a measurement for a piece of vinyl shingle, and Lou Junior says, "Yessss, dear," in the comic drone of a henpecked husband. Later, Lou Junior spins a board around and nearly knocks Al from the scaffolding. They laugh. "Your wife asked me to do that," Lou says, "but she didn't tell me how much she'd pay me."

These guys are about my age, and although they would be happy to take some down time now that the boss is off the job, I realize that I have little idea how to talk to them. Lou Junior comes into the kitchen early one morning with bundles of shingles, and when I ask him if they're hard to put up he says, "I don't know. I ain't tried it yet." We look at each other for a moment, thinking of another possible topic, but nothing presents itself. Lou Junior climbs the stairs. I stay where I am. *Good talking to you.*

They come and go—one day of work, then off somewhere else for few days, then back again. The week Lou had promised has stretched into three. But the project is getting done. On one of the last days of work, Lou Junior opens up a bit, and we stand in the empty shell of my dormer and chat about life. He asks about my trumpet playing, which he has heard me practice a few times over the weeks he's been around. "They pay you for that?" he asks.

"Yeah," I tell him. "Sometimes. Sort of."

Lou Junior looks at me as if he wants to say, *Well, now I've heard everything*, but instead he tells me of working for his father since he was just a boy—weekends and vacations and then full-time since his last year of high school.

"All I had left to finish that year was an English class and my phys ed requirement," Lou says. "So's all I had to do was go in and take the English class. Then I'd ask the coach, 'You need me today?' Most times, he didn't, so I'd go find my father wherever he was at." Now, working every day with his father, he's been building things for a living for fourteen years.

"So you never thought of going to college?" I ask him.

"Nah, not really."

"It must get pretty hard working with your father all the time," I say.

"Oh, yeah," he says quickly. There is a pause where I can tell he would be able to say a lot more, but he stops.

Then we talk about winning the lottery. He doesn't want much. "All I'm lookin' for is enough to get a little comfortable," Lou Junior says. For him that means maybe $30,000. "The first thing I'd do with that money is put enough aside to get my daughter through college."

It's the universal aim, evidence that each generation of working-class men is programmed to push its children up a different sort of ladder. I remember, when I was seventeen, my father taking me into the little closet he had converted into an office when he became secretary of his union local. He wanted to display his savings account statement to prove to me that he had enough money to put me through college. At the time, I couldn't even have guessed how much scraping, how much self-denial, went into accumulating that money, but I could sense something of the importance of it in his mind and what it symbolized to him. He pointed importantly to a figure on the bank statement. He had put aside $30,000. Without doing a thing, I had won the lottery.

Finally, they are finished.

Even before Lou Junior and Al have completed the dormer siding, my father begins putting up interior partitions in the new box, making walls for the two closets that hold either end. In the bathroom, he completes the wing wall that encloses the new bathtub. (He'd talked me out of tile and into buying a one-piece fiberglass unit that we swung into place when the big hole was opened in the roof.) Tully uses every piece of scrap wood he can find for these walls, and the result is framing that looks like someone has combined erector sets from three generations. The color of the boards varies from wall to wall, depending on the boards' age and where they had rested in the house. Some are stained with squirrel shit.

Lou Meckle notes the interior framing as he walks me through the dormer for a final inspection.

"Your father and me are kinda the same," he says. "We don't like to waste anything."

That last day of work is a sleety mess that keeps my father home watching the Weather Channel. Lou helps his son and Al load the scaffolding back into the old truck. I run down to the supermarket and buy two six-packs of beer—Bud and a microbrew sampler. As the light wanes, the three men stand with me in the basement and have a celebratory beer. To the man, they take the Bud. "I'm a simple guy," Lou Junior says, faced with the choice. I sip something called Adirondack Amber and feel like a fruit. Turns out I don't even know how to drink a real beer.

I write Lou a check on the kitchen stove for the balance of his fee, and we walk out to the deck and down into the backyard. I tell him over and over again how good everything looks.

Lou gazes up toward the dormer. A bare lightbulb we've strung is emitting a muted glow through the window.

"Well," Lou says, "I'd best be on my way." He wraps my hand in a crushing grip. "Hope ya enjoy it. It's built to last."

11.

Sheetrocking Through the Midlife Crisis

Now it is time to really get to work. The rest of the second floor will have to be gutted and the empty box filled again. First new guts—insulation, wiring, and plumbing—then a skin of Sheetrock. The three-inch, tongue-in-groove yellow pine floorboards have been coated with a dark brown stain and scarred by decades of living and the trauma of Lou Meckle's quick work. They need to be stripped and sanded and refinished. I want to raise the ceilings where I can, to give the rooms some more light and air. The new bathroom needs tiling and fixtures. It's a big job.

The weather has left me on my own a lot. My father is becoming fearful of driving in snow. "I'm here glued to the goddamn Weather Channel," he calls and tells me one morning to explain why he isn't coming up. Then he goes into his weatherman talk—lake-effect snow, storm cells, pressure fronts—and I stop listening.

This winter weather changes my life, too. For some months I've been driving into the city nearly every weekend, reversing the commute of most of the New Yorkers I know, trying to stay partially connected with my old urban life. But now, with storms sweeping in all the time, a dangerous drive for just a night or two in New York seems to be more trouble than it's worth. I figure I might as well try being a full-time Woodchuck. Over one snowy weekend I stay at the house and rip down acoustic tiles from the second-floor ceilings. Underneath the tiles are furring strips that were put up to provide a grid onto which to staple the blocks; they must come down, too. On Saturday night, after dinner on my plastic table, I climb the stairs again, pushing past the heavy green quilt we've hung to keep the heat in my downstairs living space, and prepare to pull the nails from a jumbled stack of thin boards I've torn from the ceiling that day.

The two bedrooms are nearly entirely exposed to each other; we've torn down the door frames and stripped the Sheetrock, and only the stairway divides the two rooms. The space is lit with the harsh glow of two bare lightbulbs, one in each room. To supplement these, I carry up a small metal clamp light, plug it in, and hook it onto one of the exposed roof beams. The place is brighter now, and I can look out the windows and see the skewed geometric patterns the light throws on the dark snow-covered ground in the black night. When it gets dark out here, it gets *dark*. I walk back downstairs and lug up an old radio that cost me five dollars at the second-hand furniture store in town. Just one station comes in strong and static-free: Mountain Country. One more trip downstairs to the refrigerator. I line up some beer bottles on the outside windowsill, wedged between the frost-glazed storm window and the inner glass. I take up my fancy graphite hammer and go to work.

This is not skilled labor, but as the evening lengthens and a thin, pale moon finally rises to brighten the sky like a weak night-light, I begin to feel my first stirrings of ease and comfort in work.

Maybe it's the beer. Maybe it's the sentimental whine of the steel guitars from the radio. Whatever it is, there seems to be meaning and satisfaction in this drudgery. I stack the boards on a couple of sawhorses my father made—they look like Tinkertoys compared with the Pleistocene relics Lou Meckle brought in. Is there a better way to spend a Saturday night?

Furring strips are long and thin, most of them eight or ten feet, with nails piercing the boards every eight inches or so. Tully, the king of conservation, has insisted that we save and reuse every board. So I try to pull them down intact. But no matter how careful I am, some break. Still, there are hundreds of nails, and they all have to go. I sip some beer and try to devise the most efficient way to pull them. My solution is to spread a half dozen boards across the sawhorses with the nail heads sticking up in rows, as if they were sprouts. Then, wielding the hammer, I work left to right, trying to perfect the quickest technique to extract the nails from the claw of the hammer and toss them into a cardboard trash box. Next,

I work up a system to stack the clean boards out of the way, ready to be tied and taken to the basement.

A Travis Tritt song comes on the radio. It's about a boy who has left home for the lure of the city and now, in disillusioned middle age, is rethinking his motivations. As best I can tell, the tune is called "Where Corn Don't Grow." By now it is definitely the beer. With the song in my head as I work, I begin to think of what my life might have been. Over the past several weeks, my mother has started asking me every now and then, "So, do you think you could ever be a construction worker?" I don't quite know how she means the question. Is she asking whether I could raise myself to those standards, or lower my sights?

In the refrain of the Travis Tritt song, the son asks his farmer father, "Don't you ever dream about a life where the corn don't grow?"

I remember a winter night twenty years before. I had dropped out of college, left Texas, and come back to Scranton. I was mooning around the house through what proved to be an awful January. The snow just kept falling, and the wind blew, and the drifts grew. I would put on a thick down-filled coat and a stupid-looking Irish wool hat and go for long walks in the cold, often ending up at the library of the Jesuit university across town. There I would wander through the stacks and read stuff that I picked because it seemed dense beyond reckoning, the more opaque and unintelligible the better. My reading ranged from Anaïs Nin to Noam Chomsky, and in my confusion and doubt there seemed to be no plan or purpose for this except to convince myself that I was still smart. I was planning to move to Montreal, where I could learn French and drink strong coffee. I may have had images of myself wearing black turtleneck sweaters and a beret.

All this must have worried my father. One night after dinner, he and I sat at the kitchen table, and he asked what I was planning to do, and I didn't have much of an answer. We hadn't talked that much about my going to college. I had decided on music school early in my senior year, and I applied to the two best places I knew about (the idea of a conservatory never really crossed my mind). I chose to attend the school that was a little cheaper and a lot farther from Scranton. Tully tried to convince me to enroll in the Jesuit school in town, but it was a half-hearted attempt. He didn't really know a thing about colleges.

But he knew about work. "I talked to some people," he said that night, "and if you want, I could get you in as an apprentice with the electricians union."

I knew enough about my father's world to know that this was not an insubstantial offer. Electricians are an elite on construction jobs, highly paid and mostly clean at work. Tully made the offer with the solemn tones of a father inviting his son into the Mafia. To him, being an electrician was like being a made man.

No, I told him. I didn't want to be an electrician. For some reason, I wanted to be something that I couldn't understand how to become.

"If you want to play the trumpet," he said, "you'd at least have something to fall back on."

By then I didn't really believe I would play the trumpet. Still, I told him, "I don't want something to fall back on."

Nearly two decades had passed since that night. Now I understand the good sense of having something to fall back on. I have slipped off whatever track I've been running on and feel as aimless and adrift as I had during that awful winter twenty years before. Tonight, pulling nails from boards seems utterly sane, useful, and fulfilling. Caught in the claw of the hammer, the nails make a sound like a creaky hinge. It is a comforting sound, almost as comforting as the soft twang of the guitars.

Travis Tritt sings, "I thought that I knew more then than I know now. I can't say he didn't warn me. This city life's a hard row to hoe. Ain't it funny how a dream can turn around? Where corn don't grow." I got a little choked up. There's nothing like a country tune when you're buzzed on beer and sentiment.

As I work on, the rhythm seems to get increasingly fluid, the whole process growing easier by the minute. I figure out how to use a small block of wood as a wedge under the hammerhead to make pulling the nails easier, and immediately feel so ... competent. Maybe I *could* be a construction worker.

Then I arrange a neatly stacked pile of wood and tie it with white nylon string. As I heft the bundle to head for the basement, the clamp light lunges off the roof beam and hits the floor, and the lightbulb smashes. I have tied the electrical cord of the clamp light into the woodpile. My work space is back to a harsh glare of the bare bulbs. The song is over.

If I'm going to be a construction worker, it looks like my apprenticeship is going to take longer than I thought.

. . .

The next morning, six inches of snow frost my house and everything around it. The only sound is the muffled scrape of snowplows passing.

I bundle up and push my way out the back door, shovel the deck, and then trudge heavy-footed out to the road. The state's plows and salt trucks have piled a two-foot barrier of snow and ice and salt and dirty road grime that blocks my driveway. The road is clear, but there is no way I can get to it without breaking through this hard, frozen hump.

I shovel and chop and push and strain for more than an hour and hardly make a dent. Taking a break inside, drinking coffee, I hear that peculiar roar, the inside-out muffler sound that heralds the arrival of Lurch. He is behind the wheel of a pickup truck of indeterminate origins, hand-painted flat black and probably put together with the cannibalized pieces of several dead trucks. He slows on the road, and his truck is framed in my picture window.

Lurch lowers the front shovel and plows right through the barrier, pushing hunks of the ice jam before him down toward my black walnut tree. He reverses to the road and charges in a few more times before I can get my coat and boots back on and run outside. By the time I reach the driver's-side door of his truck, the driveway is clear. Much of what used to be my driveway is dug up and pressed into the snow banks he's made.

Lurch rolls down his window, and his bushy long beard spreads itself over the sill. "I saw ya out here tryin' to shovel that stuff," he shouts over the truck's roar.

"Yeah," I yell back. "I didn't get far."

"My shovel's bigger'n yours," Lurch yells.

I have no answer to that. No argument either.

"This one's on me," Lurch says, and smiles. He throws the truck into gear and backs out of the driveway, then sets out down the road toward town with a hammering sound of pistons.

During my first winter in Narrowsburg, the length of the days stretches slowly out, like a lazy cat. Sometimes, it seems, a week will go by when a gray blanket of clouds settles ominously low over the river valley and the sun never appears. My father is as cheery as the weather. He has come out of the Christmas season in his usual manner—grumpy. He has developed his own holiday tradition, which consists of sitting in a chair, opening his presents, and saying, "What the hell is this?" or "I don't need this." My mother fixes on him a disgusted look. "*Just say thank you and shut up,*" she hisses.

At my house, as we try to work, he grows more and more distracted. He works hard, but little seems to get done. He spends the first few hours of the day walking around in circles, losing things and searching for them.

"Where's my measuring tape?" he says. "Do you have my ruler? God damn it. I'm not organized today."

He starts one job and then stops abruptly and starts on another. I have been trying not to say anything, to just go about my business, which is usually something menial. This morning, I'm putting pink Styrofoam insulation vents in between the roof rafters. They keep the blanket of fiberglass insulation away from the sheeting on the roof and allow air to flow between the insulation (which I'll be putting up next) and the roof and then out again via a vent Lou Meckle added to the ridge of the roof. This is a job my father has deemed me competent to do. He doesn't want me to wield anything more complicated than a staple gun.

Across the room, he works by himself. Except to impatiently ask me to find something for him, he doesn't ask me to help, nor does he consider that I might want to learn what he's doing. He just works. If he's using a hammer, every few minutes I hear him spit into his hands. "My hands are dry," he says.

"Did they used to be wet?"

"My skin's dryin' out. My sweat glands are gone."

Every now and then I'll hear something drop and then I'll hear him curse—"Goddamn it to hell. Son-of-a-bitchin' bastard."

Near the middle of the afternoon, he gets distracted again. It seems he's under orders to be home before dark. "Your mother's not with me today," he says. "She gets nervous."

This year they will have been married for fifty years. They now have separate bedrooms and separate televisions, but not separate lives; their lives are too small and contained to allow them much more distance from each other than a room or two. From what I can tell, they've had a successful and happy marriage, and as they enter old age together, their commitment is still strong. When they fight, though, they fight like cats—quick, scratching outbursts and then an angry but companionable silence. Day to day, in matters mundane, my mother tells me, Tully finds her responsible for everything that goes wrong. *"Shut up,"* she will whisper behind his back as he complains. They retreat into their own lukewarm video baths. He flits around with the remote control to weather, the History Channel, cooking shows. Rose watches a whole program. She is more patient, and her television is older than remote controls. Half an hour after their spat, my father will pad into her room and say, "Rose, figure skating is on." He knows she likes to watch figure skating.

Before Tully leaves for the day, he asks me again whether I have found an electrician to rewire the upstairs. I have talked to a couple of people, but the prices seemed high. And, I tell him again, "I want to do as much work ourselves as we can."

"I'm not going near electricity," he says. "I don't know anything about it. That's something I'm not going to touch. Do you know anything about electricity?"

"I'm willing to try to learn," I tell him.

"You're kiddin' yourself," he says.

When we started to tear down the walls and ceilings upstairs, we had taken down the overhead lights that hung in the middle of the ceilings and removed a few electrical plugs that were in the way. Tully had tried to rewire one of the lights to allow it to hang from the rafters, but he had shorted out the line several times before he gave up in a stream of cursing.

That night I look through my do-it-yourself manuals and figure out what is wrong. We had cut a few wires out of the circuit the light was part of, and now it sat not in the middle of a loop of electricity but at the end. This requires some simple rewiring, switching a black wire and a white wire.

At least I *think* it does. I'm not at all sure. Nervously, I spend about half an hour doing this little job that should take three minutes. As I grab hold of the wires, I have a vision of electrocuting myself. My father will find me the next morning, thrown into the corner of the room, a dead, charred lump, my hungry cat gnawing on my nose. But I get it right! The light works. I switch it on and off two dozen times to dispel my surprise and disbelief. I can barely sleep that night thinking about what my father will say when he gets to work the next day and the light is functioning.

I wait through the early morning. I don't say a word as he comes into the house and sits for a few minutes and then— "Ah, hell"—trudges up the stairs to start the workday. As he reaches the top of the stairs, I tell him, "Try the light switch." I hear the click and see the light.

"You got the light to work," he says.

"Yeah," I say. I don't quite know what I wanted him to say next, or what I wanted to explain to him. Something about trying things and not being afraid to make a few mistakes. But that's the end of the conversation.

Later that week we're downstairs in the kitchen, ripping out a piece of the countertop and a cabinet to make room for a new pipe—the main four-inch drain—which will run from the upstairs bathroom to the basement. Because of what we've added to the upstairs, we're going to have to move some walls around on the first floor. We have sawed through the countertop and pulled a two-foot section away. One whole cabinet has come off the wall. We look for a scrap piece of wood paneling to close in the side of the remaining cabinet and keep the construction dirt off my cups and dishes. I find a piece on the second floor that's nearly right—about three by six—and bring it downstairs.

"Nah," he says. "There's a better piece than this up there."

"No there isn't."

He insists on going back upstairs to look for a smaller piece that he won't have to cut. I follow him up and ask him, "Are we going to have to do everything twice—once when I do it and once when you do it again, because you assume I don't know anything?" My voice is quivering with anger. "I can tell what size a piece of paneling is."

"I'm just up here measuring," he says. That's the end of that conversation.

That night I call a friend in New York and spend an hour complaining about my father. Complaining about Tully will become a regular topic of conversation with my city friends over the next few weeks. My impatience with his impatience grows stronger every day. I feel I am about to snap under the accumulation of his persistent criticism.

One day I'm trying to move a big wad of insulation into place and I break a lightbulb.

"Aha," he calls across the room. "I saw that coming."

Later, he breaks a lightbulb. "Son of a bitch," he says. "I thought you had that light hooked up there right."

"So it's my fault you broke the light?"

"I blame you."

We're striking a chalk line in the shell of the new bathroom. He hands me the end of the line, and I pull it across to the mark he has made. I reach over and lift the string before he has fully tightened it on his end. The blue chalk blurs on the wood stud.

"Jesus!" he yells. "You never strike a line like that. Who the hell taught you how to strike a line?"

I go downstairs and make a pot of my awful coffee.

I have a small revelation. I think I remember now why I'm not a construction worker, why I went as far away from it as I could, both literally and figuratively. When you're dealing with my father, you can never do anything right. What else could I have thought during those years of my early teens, when I had the first glimmers of my future life? Construction work? Why would I have entered this game? How could I have won?

As recovered memories go, these are mild indeed. And they are vague and jumbled. But everything that's been happening over the last few weeks seems oddly familiar. I realize that my father has never been a man who could stand by and watch someone make mistakes. He wasn't tyrannical about it; my childhood wasn't a coal-town version of the Great Santini. But he has—and now I realize, has always had—no tolerance for letting someone else navigate the learning curve. My father's way of noticing an accomplishment is to point out the piece that's still missing.

I worry that I'm distilling these memories, making them stronger than the actual fact, that I am being too sensitive with his insults now that I am an adult used to being treated cordially, if not always with respect. Yet the clearer present illuminates the murky past. I see him with my nephew, his only grandson, teaching him to swing a bat with such intrusive helpfulness, wrestling the kid into submission, that I want to shout, "Leave him alone! Let him figure it out for himself!" He has made his granddaughter cry by questioning why the nineties on her report card were not *high* nineties.

I find some outside verification. Bob the Plumber watches while my father instructs me how to perform a simple operation. His lessons often begin with the phrase, "Whatever you do, don't—". Then he instructs me and instructs me and instructs me until I am so confused and frightened about doing something wrong that the only thing I can do is screw up.

"My father was exactly the opposite," Bob says one day when my father is out of hearing range. "He would set me up to do something, tell me once how it was done, and then leave me alone to make my own mistakes. That's how I learned."

"That's how people *should* learn," I tell him.

Bob agrees with me. I grant him a kind of expert status since he is now taking those college classes in education. "Tell my father that," I ask him.

He gives me a look. *Yeah, right* is what it says.

We are going to try to raise the ceilings on the second floor, which requires us to saw out the collar ties. The structure of my roof is very much like the letter A. The collar ties are the horizontal dash between the two angled strokes formed by the rafters. They add strength to the rafters and help them carry the weight of the sheeting and shingles. Internally, the collar ties provide a skeleton on which the Sheetrock of the ceiling is attached. In my house, Floyd

Campfield had set the collar ties seven feet off the floor. I can reach up and touch the ceilings, and this low roof makes the second-story rooms of this small house seem kind of oppressive. I want to take them off, cut them shorter, and reattach them closer to the peak of the letter A. When the Sheetrock goes up, I'll have a lot more height.

My father originally talked of lowering the ceilings even further. He is about five feet seven now, and shrinking. He likes to live in caves. Over the years, in his house, he'd added acoustical tile drop ceilings in several rooms, which made them quieter and helped insulate them, but meanwhile gave the rooms a claustrophobic tightness, like the inside of a jewelry box. My mother has warned me, "Don't let him lower the ceilings. He lowered all my ceilings."

The collar ties have been baking for years in an uninsulated roof (damn those sons-of-bitchin' squirrels) and, in this impromptu kiln, they've hardened into a substance that doesn't resemble any wood I've ever seen. It takes repeated pounding with hammers to work the boards away from the rafters. Uncle Santino is here today, mostly moving ladders and sweeping up. "That wood's like iron," he observes.

When the hammers aren't enough for the job, we use a small sledgehammer to pound the ties away from the rafters. Once we finally get them down, lopping off a little of each end of the boards makes the circular saw work overtime. It whines furiously.

Finally, all the ties are down and cut. We're ready to raise the roof. Tully goes to the basement to fetch his water level. Bob is working on the plumbing that day, and when he sees Tully climb the stairs with his water level in hand he can't help laughing.

"A water level?" Bob shouts. "I don't know the last time I saw a water level!"

"I think they were last used on the pyramids," I say.

"Go ahead, laugh," my father says, his thumbs stuck in either end of the clear hose to keep the water in. "But you can level around a corner with one of these. When I was doing schools, we used one of these and we could do the hallways and the classrooms in one shot."

"They use lasers now, John," Bob tells him.

"They can keep their lasers." Tully says.

Bob shakes his head and goes back to work. I hear him mutter with amazement. *"A water level."*

"Okay," my father says, handing me one end of the hose. "Whatever you do, don't take your finger off the end of this until I tell you to."

He climbs up onto a ladder and finds a measurement that will give me ceilings over eight feet high. "You're going to make the marks," he says. "That way, if it's out of level, it's your fault."

"And that's what's important," I mutter to myself. "To know whose fault it is."

"Huh?" he says.

"Nothing."

My father starts with the bubble line a little more than eight feet above the floor and holds it to a mark on one rafter. I scurry around making identical marks on the other rafters. The marks are made to his satisfaction. "Okay," he says. "Now we put the boards up." When we start trying to do this, though, the trouble we went through to get them down seems like nothing.

We can barely hammer nails into the wood. It is so hard that after a few swings, the nails simply bend over on themselves. Sometimes the head of the nail breaks off, leaving a bent body stuck in the board.

"That's not how you drive a nail," my father shouts across the room after I knock a nail head clean off. "You're hitting it crooked. Get your arm behind it, not just your wrist!"

Then he tries it himself and the nail flies off like a piece of shrapnel. Uncle Santino has to duck and cover.

"Bitch!" my father shouts. He wrestles another nail from his pouch and pounds it with a grunting fury. The first blow sets the nail. The second sends it shooting into the insulation. "Son of a bitch," he says. "This wood is like a rock."

"So, it's not my fault."

He doesn't say anything.

We spend most of the next two days fighting with these boards, making pilot holes in the wood with an electric drill and following with a hammered nail, sometimes trying to drive screws through the boards instead, though it's just as likely that the screws will bend.

"You had to have higher ceilings," my father says again and again, grunting behind the screw gun, which he takes away from me when he grows impatient with my progress. "I hope you're going to enjoy these ceilings with all you're putting me through."

"It'll make a big difference," I tell him. I've never taken particular enjoyment from a ceiling before, but I promise my father: "I'll enjoy the ceilings."

"I doubt it," he says.

. . .

Under the constant pressure, the day-to-day press of his criticism, I have come up with an analogy: My father lowered all my ceilings. What I'm remembering these days about Tully was put perfectly by a friend of mine one night as we were sitting around sipping single-malt and talking about our fathers. "What bothers me is not that he expected so much of me," he said of his father. "It's that he expected so little."

My father's words from the past few months come back to jab at me, as if they're being nailed in.

Are you going to trust his measurement?

If you don't do anything with your talent, it's your own fault.

You're dreamin' again. You're dreamin'.

If I tried, I could certainly call up other memories. I thought of a time years ago, when Tully was helping a neighbor, a man named Billy Bouacci, build his new home. Billy was a plumber straight from Italy, and he had married the younger sister of Pat Trunzo, the cop down the street. The Bouacci aesthetic was what you might call high Italian, and Billy wanted a circular ornamental plaster molding in the middle of one of his ceilings. My father had put one into our living room ceiling during one of his renovation projects. One night Tully took me with him across town to the construction site of Billy's new house, where he let me help him devise a homemade wooden compass to scribe the circle for the plaster ornament. Billy was amazed by it. "How'd you ever come up with the idea?" he asked my father.

"It was John's idea," my father said. In fact, I'd had nearly nothing to do with it, and that my father had lied to brag about me in this odd moment is as perplexing now as it was then.

Many years later, after I'd been away from Scranton for a decade, I ran into two friends of my father's at a political gala in Philadelphia, where I was playing with the dance band. This was during the time when I was making the switch from being a musician to being a writer, and though I had a full-time day job, I was still playing a lot. On a break, I went to talk with the two guys from Scranton, who told me how well I was doing as a writer.

"How did you know that?" I asked.

"That's all your father talks about," one of them said.

But this winter, it's mostly the slights I can recall. How many times have I heard my father say *You can't do that*? I'm still resentful of a morning several years ago when we were having brunch near my sister's house, in the old-town section of Alexandria, Virginia. A Dixieland jazz jam session was going on while we ate. I lamented not having my trumpet with me so I could sit in.

"You couldn't do that," my father said. I was thirty-five years old at the time, but the remark, its offhand certainty that I wasn't good enough, made me feel like he'd reached over and slapped my face. It nearly brought tears to my eyes.

"No, you're right," I said. "I couldn't." And I got up from the table and went for a walk.

Winter has almost finished slogging through by the time we are ready to Sheetrock. Everywhere, things are thawing, except between my father and me. I have begun to dread his arrival in the morning. The routine seems ridiculous.

He drives up exactly on time. I'm trying to finish the last bits of an early morning practice routine on my trumpet—calisthenics for my lips, which, as Woody Allen once said, sound like someone is sawing a trumpet in half.

I hear Tully clomp up the ten steps to my deck and push in through the kitchen door.

"What's up?" he asks.

"Nothing," I say.

He looks around and puts down the bag of groceries he always brings. He and my mother believe that I am incapable of picking out paper products or canned goods. Every week, they add to my bulging surplus of toilet tissue and string beans.

Tully sits in the plastic chair at the dining room table. He sighs heavily. "Ah, helllll."

Why do you bother? I want to ask him. *If that's how you feel, stay the hell home.* Most mornings, I wish he had. The nights are so long now, and my house so empty of distraction, that I have become more and more a regular down at the Narrowsburg Inn, where ten bucks buys a fair bit of alcohol. "Well, well, well," Lurch had shouted to me across the bar a week or so before, "you're becoming quite the drinker, quite the drinker."

Now we have forty sheets of gypsum board stacked in my dining room. More than a ton of material to replace the walls we have ripped down. All the insides—the wiring, the plumbing, the insulation—are in place, ready to be covered up. I'd hired Bob the Plumber to instruct me in electrical wiring, and he'd been an easy and patient teacher. (Of course, I was paying him a pretty good hourly wage.) I helped him run a new circuit from the basement box to the second floor, and then split off and wire for plugs and lights and heaters and fans in the bathroom. He just let me go off on my own.

"It's really pretty simple," Bob said. "If you get stuck, give me a holler. I might know what to do."

And so, with a combination of trial and error and reference to the wiring diagrams in my how-to books, I set the wiring for ceiling fans I would hang in each bedroom, a small electric heater we'd installed in the bathroom wall, and a fan-and-light combination in the bathroom ceiling. I do most of the work on the weekend, or at night, or on days when my father has stayed home. Working alone spares me the constant pressure of his instruction. One morning he shows up to find that I've wired all the new plugs on the second floor.

"You sure you got this right?" Tully says when he comes up and sees the wiring in place.

I go around with a tester to show him that every plug is working.

"You'd better have Bob check it before we close it in," he says.

"You just saw every plug work."

"Suit yourself."

We are ready to make our new walls, to close in the shell with Sheetrock. It sounds so much more rough and ready to say "We're Sheetrocking" than "We're putting up Sheetrock." When nouns become verbs, they usually gain some power and cachet.

Sheetrock is, in fact, a trademarked name, but it has come to be a generic term for wallboard, a sandwich of baked gypsum pressed between two sheets of recycled paper. I'd read somewhere that most wallboard is made with recycled newsprint. I hoped that somehow one of those four-by-eight sheets we were about to put in place would contain at least a scrap of an old newspaper article of mine, maybe the story I'd written a few years before about the world's most expensive boxer shorts. There would be some kind of poetic justice to that—a bit of my Sunday-paper whimsy made into something solid and permanent.

Our first morning at this job, we set up a low scaffold of planks and milk crates upstairs and collect the tools we will need. There's a four-foot T-square that fits over the edge of the Sheetrock and provides a straight edge for cutting the boards. Also a couple of utility knives to do the cutting, a chalk box for marking where the wood studs are, and a screw gun for screwing the boards into place. My father decides that he will do the cutting and fitting of the boards; I will be in charge of attachment.

He hands me the screw gun. "Okay, go ahead," he says. "Sheetrock through your midlife crisis."

Whenever we get a sheet cut and ready to place, he gives the order: "Okay, screw it up." I'm not sure if he means it as a double entendre.

It turns out that he doesn't have to worry about puns. I *am* screwing up. I had no idea Sheetrocking would be so difficult. Because we are working within the confines of the cozy second story of a Cape Cod, there are really no simple squares. The walls rise straight four feet from the floors and then angle over toward those collar ties we've raised fourteen inches. My father had the foresight to put the collar ties in a place that would create a strip of ceiling with four-foot span side to side. That way, one sheet will fit easily.

At least it sounds easy. But a house that has been sitting for four decades, a house whose original builders had screwed up the main support beam—that kind of house has moved and settled a bit. Those four-foot knee walls turn out to be an inch higher on one side of the house than on the other. The distance between the top of the knee wall and the newly located (and perfectly level) collar ties can change by an inch or more over a span of six feet.

We get the horizontal ceiling panels up fairly easily, but placing the sheets that will run up the rake of the roof is another story. I keep having trouble with the screw gun; the head of the bit wobbles and slips off the screw. My father stands on the floor, straining to hold the unwieldy sixty-four-pound sheet in place, doing his version of an Atlas pose, grunting with effort. I stand on the low scaffold, one hand pushing the top of the sheet in place, the other trying to position the screw and make it stick. The only trouble is that the screws fly off the bit and hit the floor, again and again.

"Jesus Christ!" my father yells. "What the hell are you doin' up there."

"I'm trying to get them to work."

"Tryin'? I'm bustin' my hump down here. Hurry up!"

Now I'm nervous. My screwing gets worse.

"For Christ's sake," he says. "*You* hold the sheet. *I'll* put the screws in."

We go back and forth like this for several days, but gradually my skill with the gun increases, the work grows smoother, and the sniping from Tully lessens. Where there was a skeleton of boards and exposed wires running like nerves, there is a smooth new skin. Finished, wrapped in the medium gray of the Sheetrock, the second floor looks good. I am enjoying my higher ceilings already.

We are just finishing the last boards in my bedroom. I have gone to fetch something in the basement, and as I climb up the last flight of stairs to the second floor, I hear my father say to Uncle Santino, "Jesus Christ, look at that. Look at that screw. He would get fired for work like that."

I push through the green blanket that is serving as the heat block. My face is flushed. My scalp feels hot and red, too.

"What's wrong now?" I ask.

"Look at this screw," my father says. Over his head, in the room that will be my bedroom, a screw is sticking down about an inch out of the ceiling. I remember that I had started it and then gotten distracted by something—I think helping my father do something else. Obviously, I'd forgotten to go back and finish that one.

"You'd get fired for work like this," he says. "When the spackler comes to work, he's going to have to stop at every screw that sticks out. You'll slow him up."

I am about to break, but I don't say anything. Does it matter? We're not working for some contractor who's watching the clock. Why can't we just do the work and correct mistakes later? It's late in the afternoon, and there doesn't seem to be any use in arguing. I've put in hundreds of screws by now, and the fact that one is sticking out an inch doesn't seem worth fighting about. Okay, I'm fired.

That night, I do what guys who get fired tend to do: I go to the pub and stay until closing time. The next morning all I can think of is a phrase my mother likes to use: "You look like you've been pulled through a knothole."

My father tells me I should organize all of the wood we've taken out of the second floor and get it ready to use somewhere else. He leaves Uncle Santino and me to do that in the basement. As we work, I hear the sound of the screw gun upstairs. Tully is redoing the screws I have put in.

Uncle Santino and I are in the damp cold downstairs, quietly working, sweeping and stacking the knotty pine that we've pulled down from the paneled bedroom. We're chatting in a desultory way, the kind of minimalist talk that constitutes conversation for my uncle. "So," my uncle has said a few times, "you could go to New York and be an electrician. They make good money."

I can hear nothing but the burring whine of that screw gun twenty feet above my head. A rage of insult and pain is swelling inside me. I feel like he's drilling those screws into my jaw.

We finally finish and go back upstairs. My father is sitting on a metal milk crate with his back to me, working on the screw gun. I have a guilty urge to hit him over the head with something. My thoughts go to another Cheever story that I've read a number of times, "Goodbye, My Brother." In it, the narrator becomes increasingly frustrated with his brother's constant complaining, his incessant finding of fault. "What can you do with a man like that?" he asks in exasperation. Finally, while they walk on the beach one day, he impulsively tries to kill his flesh and blood with a piece of driftwood.

My patricidal moment passes. Tully realizes I am in the room. He turns quickly to look at me, a little startled. Maybe he has sensed the flow of violent urges. He's wearing a hole-dotted sweatshirt and a cap that shades his liquid eyes. The flesh of his cheeks hangs in incipient wattles and shakes a little with his sudden movement. I glare at him, and the more aggrieved I feel, the more absurd our situation becomes.

I am forty years old. I have a mortgage and contribute regularly to a personal retirement fund. My hair is turning gray. Yet this project has made me regress into a person I barely recognize. I hate my father with a blind rage that has no direct cause but is simply the accumulation of a hundred perceived slights. I ache with the frustration of not feeling whole as a man, not fully in charge of my life or in control of my destiny. It is typical behavior, really. I have become an adolescent.

12.

They All Fall Down

Then my father fell down.

We were in Home Depot, the giant building super-market, which I had begun to call Home Away from Home Depot. Tully and I were buying something called Durock, a concrete-and-mesh panel that is usually used as a backing for tile in wet places—for us, the floor of the new upstairs bath-room. The stuff comes in small sheets, about half the size of a board of Sheetrock, but the concrete makes it heavy. We'd stacked four sheets onto a cart. I was finished paying and we were on our way to the door, my father ahead of me, pulling the loaded metal cart behind him. Then his feet slipped out from under him, and he toppled back into one of the cash registers and dropped to the floor.

I looked over just in time to see it happen. The motion of his fall seemed fast and slow at the same time. His feet seemed to take forever to lose their grip on the floor, but his head and shoulders fell in a flash toward the hard counter. There was no way to warn him. He didn't trip over anything. He simply fell down.

I rushed to where he was sprawled out on the concrete, figuring that by the time I reached him he would be up on his feet, laughing the whole thing off. But he wasn't. When I got to him, Tully looked up at me and seemed confused and a little frightened.

"I slipped," he said, and laughed a very tiny, wan laugh.

"Are you okay?"

"I'm not sure," he said.

It was the first time in months that I'd heard him say anything uncertain. Now I was scared.

But he pulled himself up in a moment. He had hurt his shoulder. A store manager was with us in seconds, and she sat my father down on a bench and began to speak to him as if he were a child with a hearing problem.

"ARE YOU SURE YOU'RE OKAY?" she shouted, pronouncing each word carefully. "DO YOU WANT ME TO CALL AN AMBULANCE?"

"I think we'll be fine," I told her. She was a nice woman, but her main concern, I suspected, was warding off a potential lawsuit. My father constantly rubbed his shoulder. He still seemed disoriented. Here was the guy who would let his own blood drip to the floor and continue to work, as if it were simply a pesky faucet that he'd get around to fixing some day. His slowness to rebound seemed so out of character that I felt something must be wrong.

"Maybe we'd better take you to the doctor and get an X ray," I told him. His doctor was only a mile away. We'd have to drive by on the way home anyway.

"Yeah, maybe we should," he said.

Then he told the manager that the way the workmen had poured and trowled the concrete floor was a bad idea: the surface had become too slick. "Anybody could slip and fall on that," he said. "That's dangerous." The manager's sympathy and concern seemed to dry up in an instant. My father was back to being a complaining old man. It was a good sign. Recovery had begun.

"YOU GO TO THE DOCTOR," she shouted at him, "AND LET US KNOW WHAT HE SAYS."

I loaded the Durock into my car, and we headed for the doctor.

"Did you see that floor?" Tully said in the car. "It's like glass. They used a hard trowel on that when they poured the concrete. That makes it look good. But it's like glass."

"Yeah, yeah," I said. "How's your shoulder?"

"It hurts," he said.

At the doctor's office, we walked into a crowded waiting room and Tully explained his problem. The nurse told him it would take a while for the doctor to get to him. After we'd found seats, I noticed that we were sitting near the former attorney general of Pennsylvania. He'd recently been released from a federal prison, where he'd served time for mail fraud. During that time a few years before when I was often too sad and distracted to work, I'd taken an assignment to write a long profile of this man, who was known in his hometown as Ernie the Attorney.

"I worked with Ernie," my father had told me then. "His

uncles were contractors, and he used to work for them in the summer when he was still in school."

I labored on the story for nearly a month, visited Ernie a few times, and then, in those dark days, just gave up. I hadn't talked to the attorney since his sentencing. I slid across some waiting room chairs to say hello.

Ernie was polite with me, but after I introduced him to my father, they forgot I was even there. Within minutes, Tully and the deposed politician were talking loudly about the lost art of plastering, and everybody seemed to feel better, except the other patients, who were trying to read their magazines. Our visit to the doctor took a few hours. Tully left with orders to take anti-inflammatory drugs for his shoulder and to lay off work for a while. "Ernie's havin' trouble when he's joggin'," Tully told me in the car. He'd been eavesdropping through the examining room walls.

"What happened?" my mother asked when we walked through the door, with a tone of voice that implied Tully had probably been doing something he shouldn't have been.

"I fell down," my father said.

For the next week, I was home alone. The first few days seemed like a wonderful vacation. I slept in. I read books. I puttered around, free to do what I wanted. I didn't have the old man there all day telling me what to do, telling me how I was doing it wrong, grabbing tools from my hands and doing it himself. And then I missed him.

How could I explain this? Just a few days ago we had been playing out the world's longest-running grudge match, father versus son, Laius and Oedipus at the crossroads. This was a drama too powerful and basic to ignore: Someone had to die; someone had to suffer. But somehow the script had been rewritten. One day I'd felt patricidal, the next nostalgic. All because my father fell down?

The literature of fathers and sons is understandably vast. For a while, I'd been picking through some of it, memoirs and fiction, poems and essays. I'd underline a passage here and there, jot down notes. They began to fill a file folder. The bits were random and often contradictory. Nietzsche, I'd scribbled, wrote that if you don't have a good father, it is necessary to invent one. There is a whole school of stories in which men have invented better fathers than they had in real life. And, of course, there is a very different strain of story—tales of fathers and sons who would never reconcile the inherent conflict between them. The biographers of Gandhi mention that even that great, compassionate man had a terrible relationship with his eldest son. I read stories of fathers gone missing, of fathers made mad and murderous by alcohol, of men driven to a kind of insanity by ambition for their progeny. I'd heard Arthur Miller's Willie Loman hector his sons with his delusional, pitiful platitudes. Yet nothing I came across had any strong personal resonance until I read Philip Roth's *American Pastoral.*

The fictional father in Roth's novel is Lou Levov, an immigrant from the streets of Newark who'd come up through the tanneries to find wealth as a glove manufacturer. Here was a father, Roth wrote (and as I came upon the passage, I immediately went searching for a pencil to underline it), "a father for whom everything is an unshakable duty, for whom there is a right way and a wrong way and nothing in between, a father whose compound of ambitions, biases and beliefs is so unruffled by careful thinking that he isn't as easy to escape from as he seems. Limited men of limitless energy; men quick to be friendly and quick to be fed up; men for whom the most serious thing in life is *to keep going despite everything*. And we were their sons. It was our job to love them."

What a wearying job that was sometimes. A job made harder in my case by the fact that it was a kind of work I couldn't talk about. I wasn't alone here, either. In my package of notes was a quotation from a documentary film about four young men from New York's outer boroughs who, as first-generation college students in the thirties, went on to find success as influential intellectuals. The most famous, Irving Kristol, son of a garment worker, stood near the East River, looked into the camera, and said, "I am amused to watch TV shows these days where parents go around hugging their kids saying 'I love you.' I want to tell you that never happened in the families I knew in Brooklyn. That would embarrass you if one of your parents came up and said 'I love you.' "

Nor were those words spoken in our Scranton neighborhood, two or three decades later—although, of course, the Scranton I knew was more or less limited to my own family. We simply are not a huggy bunch. And we are ridiculously easy to embarrass. So how to go about that lousy job of love?

For my father, it has always been a furious, grudging effort *to keep going despite everything*. He will rebuild this house for me whether I like it or not. Whether I like him or not. And whether he likes me or not.

And what do I do?

I think the good work is simply in the remembering. We must build monuments to our fathers in our minds, and these monuments are no less lasting than the polished pieces of stone we will surely one day purchase for them.

I had seen my father do this with his father, decades after my grandfather had died. One day, standing in my torn-up kitchen, talking with Bob the Plumber, Tully began to give one of those lectures which I suppose are for my benefit, one of those tales of how the older generation had it tough. He finds it much easier to aim these lectures at someone else, hoping they'll strike me on the rebound.

"My father took a streetcar to work in the mines," he told Bob, not me, though he'd never told me this story before. "And he'd come back at night after being underground all day, and—my God, the dirt! And half the time he'd be soakin' wet, and he had to ride that street car and walk, soakin' wet, in all kinds of weather.

"The more I think about it now, the more I feel sorry for him." As he said this, my father spread his thumb and fore-finger wide apart and held them to his eye sockets, like the pincers of a clamp, and I think he wiped a few tears away. It was something I'd never seen before. With that moment, he had entered imaginatively into his father's world, and this memory seemed more weighted with meaning than any story I'd ever heard him tell about "the old man."

There's a book by another working-class kid from one of New York's less fashionable boroughs, a guy who'd also made a name for himself in the intellectual business. I had owned Irving Howe's *World of Our Fathers* for years, but I'd never had much success reading it. Recently, as I paged through it with more purpose, I found Howe's story of his disappointment in a friend of his, another immigrant son who'd gained success as a movie producer but who, Howe wrote sadly, "could not enter imaginatively the life of his father." I had begun to think that with my father—maybe with most fathers—using the imagination is the only way we can get to know them.

For the whole time my father and I had spent together, looking for and working on this house, I had been waiting, waiting for a moment, an incident that would somehow crystallize all the furies of affection and hatred between us and allow us to know each other for the first time. The gates would spring open. We would start talking and we would be different with each other, better somehow. Now I realized those moments happen only in movies, on situation comedies—there are Frasier and his dad, huddled in an ice fishing cabin, the overeducated middle-aged son still wondering why his cop father has never hugged him and said "I love you."

That's the way it goes in TV land. In real life, Irving Howe got it right. "The distance between generations comes to be like a chasm of silence which neither affection nor good will could bridge." But this is a silence as natural and as common as the quiet of a meadow. Out of that chasm of silence between my father and me, I remember something, and try to enter it imaginatively.

I remember another time my father fell down. It happened right in front of our house, on a day that I'll imagine was crisp and bright, the kind of fall day that smells of leaves burning.

We are playing touch football on the street, one in a long-running series of games the neighborhood kids made between two telephone poles, around parked cars, the side-lines marked by a hedge here, a curb there. My father is play-ing this day. He is the last of the neighborhood fathers who comes out to play, the others having dropped away over the years. I seem to remember my mother telling him to act his age. But he won't.

It is a pass play. I may even have thrown the ball myself—I can't remember. But let's say I do, a slow, wavering spiral floating down Cayuga Street, over toward the Beynans' driveway. My father is running full out in a post pattern, being covered by a kid thirty years younger. Of course, the kid is outrun by the man, even in the tight, three-car-width confines of a normal neighborhood street.

My father catches the pass over his shoulder and turns to make the touchdown, cross the invisible goal line that runs across the street from the light pole. Just then, we all see the boy on the sidewalk, whom we had not seen before. It is Johnny Locks, a small, skinny, quiet kid who lives three houses up from ours, the last house on the street, hard by the empty flat black hill that was once a coal mine. He is a few years younger than I am, and not very athletic. He's rarely invited to play in our games. For some reason, the boy is not riding his bike but pushing it up the street.

My father sees him too late and has no time to avoid him. He crashes into Johnny and his bike, and down they go onto the sidewalk, spokes and sneakers and skinned elbows and a dull thud as their bodies hit the pavement. When every-one is upright again, somebody yells at Johnny for getting in the way. We argue about running the play over. The game resumes. Johnny goes home and goes to bed that night and never wakes up again.

Now I can remember only a few details. Did we talk about it in the house? I don't recall a word. Someone said that Johnny had fallen off his bike earlier—that's why he was walking it home—and that's how he'd gotten the concussion that killed him. I have a memory of visiting the funeral home, but it's only a flash—the skinny kid in a coffin, wearing a suit, even though, like all of us kids, he never wore a suit, his hair combed in a way he would never have combed it. Not long afterward, a couple of kids from a different neighborhood taunted me: "Your father killed Johnny Locks," they chanted. "Your father killed Johnny Locks." I wanted to fight them, but I didn't.

When I think about it, I feel sorry for him. My father, I mean, the old man, the guy who until that week had been trying his best to remain a young man. I subtract the years and realize he was my age. If I try to make the necessary but difficult effort of entering imaginatively into his life, I can only cringe. If this had happened to me, I'm not sure I would have been able to get up again. But Tully, in his way, kept going despite everything. Is it my imagination, or was that the last time he ever played ball with the kids? I run fast forward through the many days since then, and I see a man who has grown older while sitting quietly on his front porch on warm nights, his mind crowded always by the certainty that the worst thing in the world could simply come walking up the street.

I used to think that I would want to know all about that awful moment, but now I don't. Maybe Tully never thinks of it. I might be scratching at a place where only I see a scar. In the same way, neither do I wish to know what he felt when his wife lost what would have been their third child. How hard was it for him to watch while his life's work slowly went away? If he doesn't want to let anyone know, fine. In our heart of hearts, Bernard Malamud wrote once, we mourn ourselves.

Over the years, I have met a few men my age who say blithely, "My father is my best friend." That possibility once seemed like an enviable accident. Now I think I would tell them, "You don't get out much, do you?" Since I started working on this house and began a kind of extended vacation in my father's world of work, I've met several men who are with their fathers always, who have taken up their trades. It is a sweet and noble circumstance. It also seems like dancing in a minefield.

When we finally get back to work, after my father's shoulder feels better, we finish putting down the bathroom floor. We cut the Durock into the space on a T-shaped floor and fit it around the one-piece fiberglass tub and shower unit that my father insisted I buy and screw it down into the pine floors. Then Tully, age seventy-four, crawls around on his hands and knees to put cement down with a toothed trowel and starts to lay the tile. We've bought it cheap from a friend of his—leftover stuff from a commercial restroom. Life is back to normal. He wants to do all the work himself. I have to complain before he lets me help. *"Why don't I just go back to New York,"* I yell at him one night, *"and you call me when the house is done."*

In the bathroom doorway he has temporarily installed a

white marble threshold, placed to give him an edge to run the tile against. Again and again he tells me, "Whatever you do, don't step on that threshold. You'll break it."

"Okay, okay," I say. "I wasn't planning to step on the threshold."

I am making lunch when I hear a stream of cursing from upstairs. It isn't Tully's usual perfunctory cursing—there is something different about it, a tone of exhausted dejection.

He comes down the stairs and sits in the plastic chair. He rubs his face and sighs heavily. "Son of a bitch," he says. "I broke the threshold. Son of a bitch."

"You ready for lunch?"

"Oh, I don't feel like eatin' now. *Son of a bitch.*"

"We can go and get another threshold."

"I don't feel like doin' anything," he says. Tully lifts his dirty hands to his face and rubs his eyes. He looks as utterly defeated as I've ever seen anyone look.

We quit early that day. That night, lying on my futon bed, I feel sorry for him. I wonder if he'll ever come back.

The next morning, he is there as usual. A few minutes late because he has stopped to buy a new threshold. My mother is with him. She takes me aside and whispers, "He's heartbroken about that threshold. I told him, 'John understands.'"

Well, I am starting to understand. I don't know how he could have been so upset in the first place, what significance this twelve-dollar piece of marble has for him, but I do know that here is a man who would keep going despite everything.

How can you ask for more from a father? Do I want long heartfelt talks? Probably not. I'd be so embarrassed I'd faint.

Yes, I have often imagined that my life could be better if I had a different father, one who was a jazz musician, one who read books, one who could advise me on how to get along in a world where the requirements are more complex than a dirty day's work, one who couldn't care less about where to find the cheapest price for regular unleaded, one who had enough natural buoyancy that he could laugh off a broken threshold.

But watching my father fall down somehow made me forget about all that. He is what he is. And like all sons, I am what I am both because of him and despite him. One afternoon at the house, as my mother was preparing lunch, my father made another of his comments designed for but not directed at me. "I guess we've got two pretty good kids," he said to my mother, out of the blue. "I guess we've done okay."

I guess I could have done better, fatherwise, but how? Because when it comes to fathers, somehow, some way, they all fall down.

13.

Scaffold

The scaffolding goes up in the early days of the April conspiracy, as the crocuses pop out of mud cold as a milkshake and buds dot the branches of trees whose trunks still shade, here and there, a shrinking pile of snow. When it is built, I stand on top, warmed by the heat of a strong sun, yet chilled by a barrel of frigid air that rolls up from the river. From this vantage point, I have a genuine river view, and I can see huge chunks of broken ice stacked on the shore like dirty dominoes. I also feel a bursting nut of fear in my stomach, and it makes me lightheaded. I'm scared of heights.

Of all the emotions that have come unbidden during the renovation, fear has been missing so far. Every now and then, as we guide a board over the surface of a table saw, I have a strange and gut-clenching feeling that I am bound to stick my hand into the whirling saw blade. It's as if the blade pulls my hand toward it. Sometimes this pull seems uncontrollable, and no matter how much I *know* I shouldn't stick my hand into a turning saw, I feel certain I will do it anyway. Psychologists might have a word to describe this feeling. But it isn't fear exactly.

Standing unsteadily at the edge of the top tier of the scaffold—this is fear. My head is about even with the peak of my roof. That means my head is maybe thirty feet from the ground—three stories. That may not sound like much, but every time I look down, it feels like that scene in *Vertigo* in which Jimmy Stewart stares over the side of the high tower and the ground rushes upward, rising to kill him. Even in my initial, paralyzing wave of dread, I suspect that the fall would not be severe enough to kill me. Probably, I would just be hurt very badly. This seems yet more evidence of my middling existence. I swallow hard and try to concentrate my gaze on the white security of the aluminum siding.

I am holding the screw gun in one hand. With the other, I try to balance a board under my arm, which I plan to place atop a vertical pillar of the scaffold and then screw down into that board. This will provide a railing on the high side of the scaffolding, making it slightly more difficult for me to plunge three stories into the spring muck of my backyard.

"What's takin' you so long?" my father shouts from the other side of the planks, yelling over the wind. (Is it my imagination, or is the wind roaring up here?)

"Oh, nothing, just having some trouble getting this . . ."

What I want to say is *I'm scared, Daddy!*

In the last several decades, I have been afraid of many things. Playing my trumpet for musicians who are better than I provokes terror. My fears are the usual ones of the perpetual aspirant—that I will mispronounce a famous name or fall into a great gap in my social manners, that I will be discovered for what I am, the grandson of a coal miner with a thick accent. But that's a different kind of fear; *this* fear is visceral.

My father had opened the door for me to step away from this problem. During the winter, as we planned the renovation of the outside of the house—a job that required stripping the aluminum siding and then, with a bit of luck, being able to salvage and renew what was underneath—we knew we'd need to construct a scaffold. Tully had mentioned several times that it was going to consist of three levels and that if I wanted, he'd work the top level by himself. "No," I had insisted, "we'll work together." I had seen scaffolding lots of times, but I'd never actually been on it. My father had long and intimate experience with scaffolding. He knew what was in store. One day, shopping in Scranton for plumbing supplies, we came to a red light in downtown and were looking up toward the city's tallest building, a Depression-era beauty with a cream-colored terra-cotta façade. At the top, above the twelfth-floor windows and the roof (Scranton was known for its mines, not its skyscrapers; it was deep, not lofty) were panels obviously added sometime after the original construction.

"Guess who put those panels up there while hangin' over the edge on a swingin' scaffold?" my father asked.

Errol Flynn, I thought of saying, but sat mute.

"Your old man."

I squinted into the sky. It didn't seem like such a feat then, while sitting in his dirty car, which always smelled of chewing tobacco, half listening to an oldies station playing softly on the radio. At this moment, it seems like a really big deal. Twelve stories up on a two-foot-wide scaffold that hung over the edge of the roof on ropes and swayed in the wind. My father was Spiderman!

So if I'd known then, in the planning stages, what I know now during the completion, as my stomach drops like a sack of laundry through a chute, I would have told Tully, *Okay, I'll work levels one and two. You go up there yourself.*

The biggest part of the problem here is my inexperience. I keep telling myself that I'll get used to it, I'll get my "scaffold legs," and then everything will be fine. But another big part of the problem is that I have seen this scaffold rise from the muddy ground. I know how it was made and what it is made of, and that scares me half to death.

As usual, we have opted for the low-cost solution. We could have chosen to rent pipe scaffold, the Lego-like struts that fit snugly one into the other, and have been manufactured in metal to specifications which are probably detailed in multiple volumes on the shelves of the Office of Safety and Health Administration. Lou Meckle had used pipe scaffold when he cut open the roof, and it had seemed solid enough to drive one of his odd trucks onto.

Tully has decided we will build the scaffolding from the lumber we have lying around the house, like some weekend woodworking project, a birdfeeder or a bookcase. "That's all we used, was wood scaffold, when I started in construction," he assured me. Wood, after all, supported the anonymous

medieval craftsmen as they climbed toward God's holy fir-
mament and built the great Gothic cathedrals. And if it was
good enough for them . . .

A scaffold has three basic parts. The poles, the ledgers,
and the planks. Imagine a tic-tac-toe grid in three dimensions, like the celebrity boxes on *Hollywood Squares*, only in
very rough form. The first set of poles goes up vertically,
about a foot away from the outside of the house. Another set
goes up three feet apart from the first. Horizontal boards
pointing in toward the house hold the poles roughly parallel
to one another. Those boards, the ledgers, must be level
and even because they will support the planks, thick boards
that the workers walk on and work from. The poles and
the planks form the boxes of the tic-tac-toe grid. Then, for
added support, more boards are nailed in an X pattern at
the back of the scaffold to keep the poles from swaying. At
least in theory.

As we begin putting it up, it seems my father is acting
with a kind of Masonic secrecy, using code words—"poles,"
"ledgers"—that I don't understand at first. Not that it matters. He seems mostly to be talking to himself anyway. We
bought the wood for the poles back in the late fall, while we
were ordering lots of lumber from the local yard. When they
came, they were nice-looking yellow pine two-by-sixes, sixteen feet long, straight and clean. They looked like solidity
itself and made me feel impatient to build something from
them. But they spent the entire winter stacked on the floor in
the basement. Left alone there in the cold and damp, the
wood had conspired to rebel against the constraints of rigid
machine geometry imposed by the high-tech saws of the
mill; it seemed to want to be a tree again.

"Holy cripes," my father says as we pull the boards out into the spring sunlight. "They twisted like pretzels."

Actually, I would argue that the boards now look more like the standard illustration of a strand of DNA. In their bowing and twisting, they've come to resemble Watson and Crick's double helix. Pretzel or helix, it doesn't seem prudent to trust our lives to these boards.

"Maybe we should order new lumber," I say.

"Nah," Tully says. "We'll make do."

If my father has a specialty, it is making do.

I can't tell if it is habit or ideology, this propensity of his to accept what comes to him. New boards would cost less than a hundred dollars, but he would no sooner let me spend a hundred dollars (especially when I have already spent it once) than he would trade in a car every few years for another, before he'd been forced to use his own paint and brush to touch up the rust spots on the wheel wells. Is it a matter of high principle or of low self-esteem? For decades, advertisers have come at us with insidious advice and ego stroking, trying to get us to buy new stuff we don't need. *You deserve it*, they tell us over and over. My father is immune to that kind of inducement. "He just won't treat himself," my mother tells me. "He just won't." He'll make do.

Making do with something I'm going to climb up three stories on doesn't seem like a good idea to me.

Those pretzel boards have to be planted in the ground. I imagine that there is some standard, clean way of doing this, but I imagine wrong. Instead, my father drags out every old rotting plank that we've found—pieces of thick wood that look like they've washed up on shore after a long time out at sea. He drops a piece on the ground, digs around a little until it seems level, and then I wrestle a sixteen-foot pretzel over and plant it endwise onto the old board like a flagpole. Tully hammers it into the baseboard with big two-headed nails while I squeeze the board between my legs, sighting up the lumber into the blue sky.

"Is it straight?" Tully grunts.

"What's 'straight'?" I ask philosophically.

"Just tell me," he says.

I try to split the difference of the twists so that the board presents at least some surface that is parallel to the wall of the house.

"It's straight," I guess. Tully whacks the nails. Two-headed nails are exactly what they sound like they are. One head sinks like a normal nail down to the surface of the wood. The other head sticks up about half an inch, which allows you to pull the nail out again with little trouble. This is important because once we get this jerry-rigged stack of sticks up and we strip and refinish the south side of the house, we'll have to tear the scaffold back down and build it again on the north side. And then once again on the west side. Now I understood a little why the Gothic cathedrals took decades to construct.

With one pole up, we cut up a few short pieces of furring strips (the ones I'd cleaned to country music and beer months ago) and nail the pieces at an angle, one end in the pole and the other into the side of the house. Tully breaks some sticks into short pieces and hammers those into the ground around the baseboard, like tent stakes. This is supposed to keep the base from shifting. Now the pole stands on its own, just about. Seven more to go.

I have learned a little about how my father's mind works over the months we've spent together. If he is going from point A to point G, it is a ride on the local. He will stop all along the way and visit points B, C, D, E, F. I'm not sure whether he developed this habit while learning his trade— any manual skill requires doing things correctly and in the proper sequence—or whether he was born with it. In any case, it spills over into his view of the world and the way he expresses it.

If I had been listening more closely, I would have seen this years ago. One of our favorite summer games was eating cold watermelon over the kitchen sink, him on one side, me on the other. We'd turn the tap on and spit the seeds into the sink and watch them spiral with the water down the drain. Then my father would begin his spiel.

Okay, the seeds are down in the basement now, and now they're out to the street. They're going down the sewer pipe. Now they're in front of the Trunzos' house. They're down to the Dolans'. They're at the bottom of the hill. They're making the turn on Brick Avenue. This detailed literalness seemed endlessly amusing when I was a kid.

Lately, though, when Tully tries to explain to me what he wants done, he includes so many details that by the end of his speech I've forgotten his point. One day he tells me about a vacation he and my mother had taken together years before, a road trip on old two-lane highways. "That's when I had the Chevy," he says. (He references chunks of his life by the car he was driving at the time.) He remembers every town they stopped in, every road they were on, and he recites them to me, in order. He probably could tell me every meal they ate, but I distract him by asking questions about the end of the trip. "So where'd you stop *just* before coming home?" What I want to do is say, *Please, please, please get to the point of the story.*

While we were finishing the upstairs bathroom, my father took a long time to set the new doors. He was insistent that they be exactly plumb, a process that takes a lot of jiggling and shifting, working with shims in a ponderous game of cards. When he finished, he called me over to show me the results of this carefulness.

"If you open the door to here," he said, pushing the door about three inches open, "it stays there."

He moved the door three more inches. "If you open to here, it stays there."

He moved the door several more inches. "If you open it to here, it stays there." By now I'd gotten the gist of it—a level door stays where it is positioned, not like most doors, which swing shut or creep open seemingly of their own accord. I grabbed the door and moved it a half inch back toward him.

"What if I open to there?" I said.

"It stays."

I moved it another eighth of an inch back. "How about here?"

Tully looked at me and realized I was teasing him. "That's right," he said. I guess I should have told him he did a good job hanging the door.

All I can say is that it's a good thing that my father's literal and deliberate mind is in charge of our scaffold design.

If I were to climb to the top of a swaying assemblage of wood that I'd devised, trembling would be added to my fear.

The motley collection of boards, planks, pieces, nails, and furring strips somehow, following Tully's plan, takes shape and ascends the south side of my house. Where the unevenness of the ground makes planting the poles difficult, my father hauls out a rotting wooden platform we found in the basement when I took occupancy of the place. We prop it level with stones and pieces of other boards. The whole thing begins to look like a treehouse built by some particularly eccentric self-taught architect. Somehow, the collection of new and old, straight and crooked pieces becomes a structure whose whole is indeed greater than the sum of its twisted parts. We get all the poles standing and then secure the first row of ledgers. Wrestling with long two-by-twelve planks, we set up the first base and climb onto it to test its solidity. It holds! Bootstrapping from that level, we build the second. There is something antlike about the progress we make, hauling electrical wires, drills, and buckets of screws and nails along with us. The second set of ledgers goes up more easily than the first. Then a few more planks go into place, and we have a second level. From there we put up the third story, a high perch about the level of my second-story windows.

It stands, too, holding two overweight men. Although it sways a little and I imagine that at any minute those ugly pieces of scrap wood on which everything sits will disintegrate and bring the whole pile down, there we are, thirty feet off the ground, me shaking with fear, my father seeming to enjoy my predicament a little too much. We've built a scaffold.

"Don't give away my secrets," my father says.

Not to worry.

It is time to peel off the aluminum siding. Like so many other things we've done, this seems like a simple job until it comes time to do it. This needs to be careful demolition work. Once you get in the mood for demolishing stuff, "careful demolition" becomes something of an oxymoron. We've determined through a couple of test spots that the original wood siding is a fine red cedar—the kind of stuff, Tully is fond of saying, that would cost a fortune to buy these days. The aluminum covers the wood siding in overlapping rows and is attached to it with hundreds and hundreds of nails, which will need to be delicately removed to keep the siding from splintering. We work in the opposite direction of the original installers, removing the sheets of metal from the top, from the little triangular piece under the peak of the roof, down the widening strips that stretch to ten or twelve feet in length near the foundation. This is frustrating work, trying to get a pry hold under the aluminum with the claw of the hammer, gently coaxing back the end to start the nail sliding out, then pulling each nail slowly to avoid shredding the wood underneath.

At one point we are sitting on the planks of the highest level, warming in the sun, sweating from the effort. We've stopped after a long piece of aluminum peels off and drops to the ground. Our feet dangle beneath us as if we're kids on swings.

"I spent a lot of my life like this," Tully says. "Up on a scaffold like this."

"Did you like it?" I ask him.

"It made money."

I am starting to give up on the idea that my father will ever display an emotion other than impatient frustration. His hands, scarred and scabby, are more eloquent about his life than he is. The closest he's come to betraying anything other than a practical sense was months ago, as we drove through the farm-flecked hills of Wayne County toward Scranton. The car climbed to the top of a ridge that opened to a wide rural vista, the fields forming softly rounded geometries traced in green and brown, the sky streaked in primary colors in the early fall evening.

"It's a beautiful sunset," Tully said in a particularly uncharacteristic burst of aesthetic passion. But then he caught himself and added quickly, "If that's worth anything."

Now that we're up on a scaffold, Tully is a happy man. It gets even better when all the aluminum is down. I treat us to a new gadget—a power washer—and Tully takes to it like a boy with a new toy.

The idea behind the purchase is to save us the trouble of scraping the paint off the wood siding once we've removed the aluminum wrapping. A power washer is a water pump that you run your garden hose through. Using a small two-stroke engine, it builds up pressure of several thousand pounds through a nozzle on the end of a gunlike wand. I'd seen one of the guys on a home repair television show using a power washer, and the paint on the old house they were fixing peeled away like the flaky skin of a summer sunburn. For weeks after I bought it, I couldn't get through a telephone call to a city friend or a gathering around Narrowsburg without blurting out, "Well, I got myself a power washer." It seemed like the final piece of evidence I needed to convince myself that I actually owned a home.

Once we get the new tool up and running, I don't exactly warm to the joys of power washing. The washer is an infernal machine, noisy as hell, as if all your neighbors have decided to mow the lawn at the same time. And while the pressure spray does lift the paint right off the wood, it doesn't work as cleanly as I've seen on that television show. Certain patches of paint cling tenaciously, and if I hold the spray on them too long, the hard stream will actually eat a hole in the wood. Red cedar is not a hardwood.

Plus, I have to wrestle the hose and pressure wand to the top of the scaffold and work up there by myself. I'm getting my scaffold legs and feel a grinding terror only every few hours or so. But aiming a pressurized stream of water, being careful not to let it linger, trying to see through the resulting mist and not step off the edge of a plank—that gives me too much to think about at once. I do the two top levels, working downward, and am frazzled and worn out. I hand Tully the wand. He takes it with great dignity and seriousness and then works on the lower siding with a precision that seems surgical.

In the days of power washing, I learn a few more things about my father that surprise me. Whenever we shut the machine off to move it to a different place or prepare to attack from a new level of the scaffolding, I have to start the machine up again. It has a pull rope just like a grass cutter, and Tully doesn't have the strength to pull it hard enough to get started.

We move to the the front of the house. This is closer to the ground, and the low end requires only a short, portable scaffold to reach its highest point. Here we use ready-made A-shaped metal braces with a board clamped between them, sort of like an oversized sawhorse with planks on top. I have to carry around the metal braces we use as ledgers. My father gets under one early on and can't raise it from the ground by himself.

It never occured to me that a day would come when I would be stronger than my father. At first I felt a flush of pride, and even a little arrogance. "I'll get it," I say pompously, pushing past him to lift the horse and lug it across the front yard. But somehow I realize that this shift isn't an accomplishment. It is a loss. My father is fading, and I am going to have to carry more of the load. I don't know if I feel quite ready to assume the heavy lifting.

After we have used the pressure spray to take off as much paint as possible, we scrub the walls with Spic 'n' Span. I don't know why, exactly, but my father's painter friend had told him to do that. I scrape and scrape and scrape. Spring has come, and the air is fragrant with growth, cool in the mornings and lullingly hot by the afternoon. We begin to take our lunches outside. My father works happily on other jobs—he doesn't like to scrape. One day he stands at the base of a scaffold, under where I've transformed a patch of the wall from grimy white to the burnt umber of the cedar. The pungent smell of the wood hangs in the air. "Look at that wood," he says. "You can't buy wood like that these days. It's beautiful. It's a crime what they did to this house."

Uncle Santino begins to show up twice a week. Following my progress, he carefully sands every inch of the siding that he can reach without climbing the high scaffold. The burring drone of his palm sander makes a comforting background noise. I add a fragmented melody of steel on wood, a steady staccato theme like violinist gone mad. Tully provides percussion with hammer blows as he fixes the aluminum trim that remains around the edge of the roof.

Painting a house can be tedium itself. It is cathartic that way, almost a form of meditation. With each pull of the scraper, it seems I am taking off a layer of the excresence of my life, the resentments and grudges and misunderstandings floating to the ground in flakes. I shrug off the discontent of winter like a heavy coat and am glad to be rid of it. There are mornings when I can't wait to get up on the scaffold and work in the early chill. The collection of twisted boards and rotting planks becomes in the new light of a soft morning my own jungle gym, and, confident now, I climb onto it and around it, pulling myself past corners, leaning out over the edge sometimes for the sheer joy of leaning.

Settling in to work, I swing my legs from the plank where I sit and concentrate on nothing more complex than a length of board. This is gratifying work, with an obvious and simple strategy and visible results. When we finally get the brushes out and start painting—two coats of oil-based primer and two coats of latex finish—the difference is immediate and remarkable. The house seems to be suddenly transformed. The ugly stepsister has stepped into a beautiful ball gown.

By now I have learned how to dip a brush, tap the edge of the can, and pull up a rich, milky brush full of color. When I sweep it back and forth across the scaled surface, the change is magical.

For weeks we work like this. The scaffold comes down from the south side and grows, stick by stick, on the north side. The days get brighter and longer, and some afternoons the air becomes as soft as the petals of a flower. When the part of the house that faces the road is done, my father stands off in the driveway and surveys the results.

"Now, that looks like a million bucks," he says.

14.

John and Tully's
Excellent Adventure

I've made a mental note to tell Bob Vila my idea for a new home repair show for television. Bob Vila, of course, is the guy who for ten years hosted the phenomenally popular program *This Old House*. You might say he singlehandedly invented the genre of how-to home repair on television. At the very least, he was present at its creation.

My idea for a home repair show is based on the experiences of a man who has recently turned forty, someone who in all those years never found time to learn how to hammer a nail. The guy buys a fixer-upper in the country and sets out to totally renovate the place himself, under the tutelage of an old man who has spent most of his life as a construction worker. My show would focus on the basics: learning to use a hammer, sawing a board straight, not driving quarter-inch drill bits through your thumbnail. The title I have in mind comes from a phrase that would be shouted repeatedly by the seventy-five-year-old construction guru.

The opening of the show would feature a snappy theme song. Fade the music, and up comes the professional announcer. "It's time once again for . . ."

Then Tully's voice: "DON'T DO IT LIKE THAT!"

I have lots of time to fine-tune my concept during the eight-hour drive from Scranton to the elbow of Cape Cod. Interstate 95 through Connecticut is an ideal place for daydreaming. Tully is in the passenger seat. We're on a road trip.

A few days ago, the phone rang in my kitchen just as the sun was going down, hours after we had finished working and Tully and Santino had left for home. It was an editor from the *New York Times* calling to tell me how much she liked a short essay I had sent her. It was about planting trees in my front yard, and about how I worried that those thin little hemlocks wouldn't survive their first winter. She wanted to run it.

We started talking about story ideas I might have for her, and that's how I ended up driving to visit Bob Vila. "I think you really need to bring your father along," said the editor, who now knew about my renovation project with Tully from reading my tale of the hemlocks. "We can call the story 'John and Tully's Excellent Adventure.'"

I tracked down Bob Vila as he was filming a television commercial in Portland, Oregon. When he got on the phone, he was sitting in a dressing room waiting to walk on the set ("That's my perky makeup girl knocking on the door," he said at one point). Bob said he'd be happy to get together. When he wasn't filming commercials for Sears tools, he was spending the summer at one of his four (or five, or six—I never was able to pin him down on a number) homes. He told me that when he finished shooting in Portland he was heading back to the summer "cottage" he'd built in the Cape Cod town of Osterville, just down the road from Hyannisport. He built it not long after he and *This Old House* parted company. Vila and his public-television bosses had had a complicated dispute that centered on his very lucrative side career endorsing various home repair products. In those more innocent times, Vila's growing prominence as a pitchman seemed to violate the spirit of public broadcasting, and he and *This Old House* had an acrimonious split. "I figured it would a good time to get out of Boston," Vila told me.

"If you come out next Wednesday, I'm having a cookout," he said. "That would be more fun than an interview, wouldn't it?"

"Can I bring my father?" I asked.

"I have no problem with that," he said.

So I broke the news to Tully that he had an assignment from the *New York Times*. He actually turned down the volume of the Weather Channel.

"What the hell do they want to do that for?"

"I don't know," I said. "But they really want you to come along."

"For what? Nah, I don't think so."

"They know that we're renovating this house together," I said. "I think *they* think it will be funny to have a real construction worker meet Vila."

"What am I gonna do?"

"Whatever you want."

Tully thought for a minute or two. "I guess I could do it," he said. "It sounds weird to me."

"It'll be fine," I said. "It might be fun to meet Bob Vila, don't you think?"

"He seems like a pretty nice guy," my father said. "You know, I think he's the best of all those guys that do those TV shows." Even with the promise of free grilled food, my father is not the kind of guy who throws around compliments. But like millions of other Americans, he had seen Bob Vila on television and liked what he saw. Being from the generation that watched TV grow from nothing to a controlling influence in our lives, my father trusted and admired—felt awe for—anyone who appeared on the tube. Tully had started watching the renovation programs soon after we started looking for my house. "They got one," he informed me once, "where a guy and girl work together. And she does just as much as he does."

But to Tully, Bob Vila is the guy. He is the Milton Berle of the home repair shows. And he has transcended the early-Saturday-morning ghetto where those programs usually dwell and become something of a pop culture icon. Vila is a spokesman for Sears Craftsman tools. For years, he appeared regularly on NBC's *Today* show, where he taught those busy homeowners Bryant Gumbel and Katie Couric how to build essentials like toy boxes, entertainment centers, and picnic tables, and how to fix their leaky faucets. (As if that would ever happen.) Vila voiced his opinions on the late-night talk show *Politically Incorrect.* He had guest-starred as himself on the prime-time hit sitcom *Home Improvement,* a show in which Tim Allen plays someone a lot like Bob Vila. Lately, he was doing his own syndicated home repair show and a series he developed for one of the cable networks called *Bob Vila's Guide to Historic Houses.* This is a guy with wide and constant exposure. I talked to a Sears marketing executive about Bob Vila's worth to them as a salesman of tools. "Bob has really good Q-scores," he told me. "Q-score" is advertising lingo for a research quotient of on-screen likeability. "From the most recent surveys we've done," the Sears guy added, "Bob Vila is recognized by seventy-three percent of all the living, breathing adults in America."

One of those adults is my father.

"You think we'll get some free tools?" Tully says, sometime after we've crossed into Rhode Island.

"I can't take any free tools," I tell him. "I'm a journalist."

He stares out the passenger window for a moment and I can almost *hear* his mind working. *"I'm* not a journalist," he says.

What has really sparked the interest of the *New York Times* is the fact that Hearst Magazines is getting ready to ship out issues of *Bob Vila's American Home,* a glossy new publication that will try to meld the gritty advice of men's how-to magazines with the highly styled dream-house photos that have long been the staple of women's shelter books.

I've seen some early test issues of Bob's magazine. From the cover photos of a smiling Vila in a workshirt to cover lines that included "Bob's Perfect Patio" and "How We Got Our House on Bob's TV Show," it was a publication that was selling celebrity as much as home repair advice.

Before I left for Cape Cod, I had talked with John Mack Carter, Hearst's director of new magazine development and the former editor of *Good Housekeeping*. "We really hadn't exploited the area of celebrity and expertise," he told me. "I had considered several experts in different areas, but Bob stood out." Carter used the phrase "exploitation of expertise combined with television exposure" and quickly compared Bob Vila with the paragon of synergy in the multimedia life-style advice business: Martha Stewart. Since I'd started renovating the house, I'd been tempted only a few times to buy a copy of *Martha Stewart Living*. Reading it was like strolling through a perfectly lit dream world where you might live if only you were only a million times more fussy and competent than you really are. (It would also help if you had as many harried assistants as Martha does.) I became intrigued by the idea that Bob Vila could rival Martha Stewart. In our first telephone talk, Vila downplayed the comparison. But he was quick to add, "It's inevitable, isn't it?"

Imagine a marginally more relaxed Martha Stewart with a beard. Is America ready for that?

Bob Vila is moving around his huge, impressive kitchen, dressed in sandals, khaki shorts, and a tan Lacoste shirt, supervising the preparations for a summer seashore cookout. His dinner guests are helping. Asparagus stems are being snapped, swordfish steaks are marinating, fresh clams are steaming in vermouth. Bob asks me to slice some eggplant and then warns, "Do it fast, I move very quickly." My father is lurking on the fringes of the action. When Tully sees me pick up a big expensive knife and start chopping, he can't keep himself from laughing. Mostly, though, he is eyeing the polished granite countertops and not one but two industrial-strength cooktops. The stoves alone would blow our entire kitchen renovation budget.

Bob's wife is working, too. She is a small, attractive woman named Diana Barrett. She teaches at Harvard's School of Public Health. Bob and Diana have been married for twenty-two years and have three children, the oldest of whom is going to turn twenty-one in a few days. "I put away a really lovely bottle of wine the day he was born," Vila told us as he emerged from his basement wine cellar with to-night's vintage. "We're going to drink it together on his birthday." I can't imagine Tully even thinking of such a gesture. And even if he had, the twist-off cap would probably have rusted after all these years. Until now, I have been skeptical of Mr. Vila beyond even the normal standard of a working journalist. But this makes me begin to like him.

Tully and I first met Vila earlier at the offices of his production company, a clapboard building on a cul-de-sac not far from his home. Vila is friendly and hyperactive and completely distracted as I pull out a tape recorder and try to start an interview. After just a few minutes of scattered talk, Bob hops up from his chair and says, "Let's get out of here." He tells Tully and me to follow him home, and I have to violate a half dozen traffic laws to keep up with him as he races along in a huge, shiny Mercedes sedan. That morning, Tully had been nervous as a cat at the thought of meeting a celebrity, but now he's loosening up. "That's some place he's got back there," my father says as we swerve along the narrow Cape Cod roads from Bob's office to his house.

We reach Sand Point, what Vila ironically (but quite accurately) calls his compound, two large homes and a guest cottage that sit right on the water. We pass through a gated guardhouse on the way in and park near the guest quarters. As we walk toward the main house, Vila stops and turns to look at my Honda Civic.

"Whose car is that?" he asks. He obviously hasn't been keeping an eye out for me in his rearview mirror.

"That's mine," I tell him.

"Oh," Vila says. "I got confused there for a minute. My housekeeper has a car like that. But this is her day off."

Tully is obviously impressed by the house. The main building is geometrically complex, with a pair of two-story octagons linked by a bridge that crosses a cathedral-like great room. The back of the house communes with the water via an L-shaped covered terrace and a screened-in dining porch. A long wooden pier leads out to Vila's private dock. In front is a sunken garden in a conservatory, which was built with the *Home Again* cameras rolling. That episode included a guest appearance by Martha Stewart herself, who helped Bob's wife buy plants and then served tea in the new structure.

"I could tell you what I thought about Martha," Diana says. "But you'd have to assure me that it would be off the record."

"I'd rather not," I say.

She can't resist. "Well, let's just say that she's not the warmest person you'll ever meet," she tells me. "But I'd rather you didn't use that."

As the cooking preparations continue, Diana vies with her husband for control of the kitchen. They have short, cheerful arguments about preparing the food; mock, playful fights, which sometimes end with Vila, a Florida native of Cuban heritage, exclaiming in Spanish. It seems to be a well-worn routine. Watching her husband's celebrity grow has left Diana bemused. She mentions a recent promotional appearance Bob made for Sears.

"If you had told me twenty years ago," she says, "that my husband would be cutting a cheesecake in half with a reciprocating saw—I don't know what I would have thought."

Dinner, Vila decides, will follow a late afternoon cruise aboard his thirty-two-foot gentleman's version of a Maine lobster boat. "You're comfortable on the water, I hope," he says to Tully.

"I should be," my father says. "I spent twenty-one months on a ship in World War II."

"Oh, really," Vila says, the tone of boredom in his voice almost palpable.

Vila coaxes his boat alive, and with a sputtering roar we sail into the channel protecting the exclusive island where he resides. The *Times* has hired a photographer to come along, and he is busy running around, as photographers do, sticking the camera over Vila's shoulder, pointing it in his face.

"I would really appreciate it if you didn't take pictures of any of my neighbors' houses," Bob tells him. "I'm a public figure, but most of them are a lot richer than me and a lot more concerned about their privacy."

As sensitive as he is about the pampered image his community's guardhouse projects, it quickly becomes apparent that Bob Vila is a man who gets great satisfaction from a lifestyle that is far removed from that of most folks who wear tool belts.

We putter around the waters, ogling the expensive homes, Vila occasionally dropping a famous name—Kennedy especially. He offers to let us drive the boat, and I take him up on it for a little while. Tully, the sailor, declines.

"Unfortunately," Bob says, "there's been a Hollywoodization of this town in the last few years. People are starting to come in and knock down two-million-dollar houses to make room for five-million-dollar houses." Vila points to one of these expensive new waterfront homes, a rambling "cottage" with a mélange of dormers, turrets, and rooflines. "That architect has designed a number of the new houses around here," he says. "If it was up to me, I'd get her banned."

Though Vila won't name the architect, calls I later make to local building officials lead me to a woman named Doreve Nicholaeff, who admits to having designed several very large houses in the area, including one currently under construction for the chairman of General Motors. At first she is shocked by the call, and nervous. I explain to her that the newspaper, in its strict policy of fairness, would not allow her to be criticized without giving her space to respond.

"Why would someone like Bob Vila pick on me?" she asks incredulously. "He could really hurt my business. He has no idea what he's talking about." She starts to loosen up.

"I have some very prominent clients who obviously like what I do," she says. "My houses are designed to be very site specific and sensitive to the environment, which are qualities I don't find in Bob Vila's house."

"Thanks," I say. "That's exactly what I needed." But now I can't get her off the phone. She continues the interview on her own, telling me how her young daughter attends school with Vila's. "He's such a snob," she says. "He drives around in his fancy cars and looks down on anyone who isn't as rich as he is. You can ask anyone."

I don't feel the need. Simply listening to Vila's officious pronouncements on the local architecture shows me that he is no longer a guy content to renovate old houses on TV. He wants to be a tastemaker. He went into home renovation in the seventies with unusual credentials—a degree in communications, two years in the Peace Corps, and a short stint studying architecture. "I was twenty-seven, just back from Europe," he tells me. "I bought a truck for five hundred dollars, bought some tools, and had some cards printed with my phone number saying I did antique house restoration."

His first job was restoring the picket fence of a house next door to the Cambridge home of Julia Child. A strange coincidence, since a few years later he would be plucked from obscurity by the public television producer Russell Morash, who had more or less invented the how-to program in the sixties with Ms. Child's *French Chef* series. Vila likes to remind people that he was paid $250 per episode when he signed on with *This Old House*. He quickly learned that the real money was in endorsements. And the popularity and critical success of *This Old House*—it is a perennially top-rated PBS show and has won fourteen Emmys—gave him a high level of authority and recognition.

How much of his own authority Vila brought to the mix is subject to some debate. I kept trying to interview Russell

Morash, and he kept ducking me. Finally, he told an assistant to tell me that he just wouldn't talk about his former star anymore, he was sick of it. But I tracked down a story in the *Los Angeles Times* in which Morash spoke on the subject of Bob Vila.

"He had a glib way about him," the producer was quoted as saying. "Didn't know anything about building or contracting or anything else. But he was certainly a talker."

Another journalist friend of mine sent me a story he'd written some years ago about Vila, which detailed the time before he became a TV star. After completing a handful of restorations around Boston in the early Seventies, Vila was cited by *House Beautiful* magazine for renovating his own home, and that caught Morash's attention. In addition to the awards, there had also been a couple of lawsuits against Vila for his renovation work. One came from the owner of a town house in Boston's historic Back Bay district who claimed Vila's rehabilitation had violated local historic preservation rules. More recently, Vila was sued by an actor who bought a Malibu house that was refurbished for the *Home Again* series. He was disappointed in the workmanship.

Over the course of the day, I keep trying to get Bob to discuss the lawsuits, but he keeps declining. "Both cases have been settled," he finally tells me impatiently, "and that's all I'm going to say about them." I was learning that the friendly, just-folks Bob Vila that we see on TV can quickly turn curt and sarcastic.

Dinner is finally coming together. The swordfish is sizzling on a high-end outdoor gas grill as the sky over Oyster Harbor begins its polychromatic descent to darkness. We're sitting on the stone terrace just down the hill from Bob's mother-in-law's house.

"You'd better hide," Vila tells my father. "If my mother-in-law sees that we've got someone here with white hair and we didn't invite her, she'll be really angry at me."

Tully blushes.

We talk for a while of Bob's son. "He's studying art," Vila says. "I keep telling him that it's a really tough field, and he ought to have something else to fall back on."

"That's what I told John," Tully says. "Back when he was a musician."

"Well, look," I say. "It worked out."

"So," Bob's wife says, "you fell back on writing for the *New York Times.*"

"I guess you could say that."

"What you and your father are doing reminds me of me and my dad," Vila says. "He built a house himself out of concrete blocks in Miami when he needed a place for his family. My earliest memories are of him working on that house—it was always being added to. When I was thirteen, I helped him put on a new roof." Vila points to a bridge near the water. He and his father built it together not long before his father died.

Earlier, I'd tried to turn the conversation to my house project. I know by now that if you get your house featured on a program like Vila's, free stuff begins appearing from manufacturers who want their names on TV.

"You got a house you're renovating," Bob said then. "How did I guess. Get in line. We get so many submissions you wouldn't believe it." (I figured it wasn't a good time to mention the idea for a TV show with Tully and me.) When I told him my house was near the Delaware River in Sullivan County, New York, he was even less interested.

"If I have to get on two planes and then drive," he said, "forget about it." Bob turned the conversation back to the new set of Sears tools for which he'd recently filmed several television commercials. He had just happened to leave a package of the tools—drill bits and screwdriver heads which could be quickly alternated on a driver—lying around, and my father fixed a covetous look on it. But nobody made an offer. Tully would just have to continue to borrow tools from his old union buddies.

As we load our plates with food and gather around a candlelit table in the screened-in dining porch, I begin to realize that with his many commitments, Vila has little time for anything but being Bob Vila. Even his how-to television show has been weighted heavily toward how he's improved his own rarefied lifestyle. The season before our visit, the programs focussed on the renovation of his main home, in Cambridge, where his neighbors include Alan Dershowitz and Yo-Yo Ma. For the upcoming season, he has filmed thirteen segments on the renovation of a modest kit house on very pricey property in Los Angeles. The next thirteen weeks will be devoted to the eighty-foot car-and-boat barn Vila is building for himself on the Cape Cod cul-de-sac where he built his office building and a home for his housekeeper, the one who drives the same car I do.

Though I am less and less impressed by Vila as the night wears on, I can tell that Tully loves the guy. My father has never been a guest in a place like this. "I never had swordfish before," he confesses at one point. Tully is a blue-collar guy who thinks that financial success indicates virtue. He's not alone there.

When I spoke to John Mack Carter, he said an interesting thing about Vila: "I think he invented Bob Vila because of a certain frustration and unfulfilled impulse he had. He went into construction to pay the bills and put food on the table. His name and personality and his satisfaction with buildings are all expressions of his personality. Bob Vila was built stick by stick. We could well study him for that ability."

During our visit, Vila has described himself in several different ways. "I'm eighty percent a real estate developer," he says at one point. "I'm an entrepreneur at heart," he says at another. Once he even leans back in his chair, sips some nice white wine, and states self-importantly, "I'm a pop figure." Vila happily reports that the folks who make their living from him like to call him "The Franchise."

Dinner is good. The fish is terrific. The corn is sweet. The eggplant I have cut is burnt to a crisp. I had started to cut it thick, but Bob insisted on thin slices, and they couldn't handle the heat of the grill. "I saw that comin'," Tully whispers to me. "He had you cut them too thin."

Finally, as we sit around the table after dinner, our talk somehow turns to satellite television. I have my opening. I pull out a photo of the twelve-foot satellite dish that came with my house, the one that is now obsolete and an ugly garden ornament.

"What would you suggest doing with this?" I ask.

"I've got it," Vila says, grabbing the photo. "You make a gazebo out of it. Take the dish, turn it upside down, put some lolly columns in the ground, and bolt the dish onto them. Then let some vines grow up around it."

An impressed murmur goes around the table at Bob's quick idea. Satisfied, he gives me the photo back.

"I wanted to make a gazebo out of it," Tully adds quickly, with a distinct tone of pride in his voice. "I told him that's what he should do with it." I don't have the heart to tell Tully that in an earlier phone conversation, I told Vila about the satellite dish and the gazebo idea. The TV star is just giving me back a reading of my own script.

Soon dinner is over, and my father and I get up to leave. On the way out, Bob takes us on a quick tour of the house. "It was framed by Norm Abram," he says, declaring a quick, unilateral truce with his former colleague from *This Old House*. "He's a really good carpenter."

But carpentry seems the last thing on Vila's mind. He is more interested in showing us the beautiful objects he's collected and salvaged—glassworks from Italy, a Gioponte chandelier, doors from Morocco—all of which display his impeccable taste.

Tully politely eyes the expensive knicknacks, but he's more interested in the structure. Of course, he finds the one visible fault, a large crack running down a wall.

"What's that?" Tully asks. "Blue board?"

"Yeah," says Vila. "We had some pretty good guys doing it, but you know, you just can't stop cracks."

"Sure you can," Tully says.

Soon they are discussing plaster techniques and corner beads and king poles. I leave them alone and step into the powder room. There's a copy of *Martha Stewart Living* in the trash can.

We're in the car, heading away from Sand Point, when my father says, "That Bob Vila seems to have learned a lot. I don't know if it's all an act or not."

"What about Bob's gazebo idea?" I ask, knowing that my father had decided to make the dish into a gazebo the first day he saw it.

"Yeah," Tully says skeptically. "I wouldn't do it like that."

15.

Chalk Lines

I have gone into the basement to replenish my supply of wire nuts. On the way back up the stairs I hear my father say to Bob the Plumber, "I had him up and down that scaffold. He's a climber now."

"Boy, I'll tell ya," Bob says, "I didn't recognize the place when I drove up. It looks like a different house."

All my climbing today is simply up and down the flight of stairs to the basement, where the main circuit-breaker box occupies a dark corner. Several long tails of wire dangle out of the box. I'm running new electrical circuits into the kitchen for lights and plugs and appliances. My father has come to accept that I have figured out the basics of wiring, and he lets me alone as I work.

Tully has even asked me to come to his house and run a new circuit in what he calls his "shed" in the backyard. It is hardly a shed, but actually a little house with windows and plaster walls, resting on a concrete slab that was once our backyard patio. Since he built it, fifteen years ago, I have always called it Fort Tully.

When I arrive to do the wiring in his fort, Tully has everything ready for me, including the tools I will use and the wire. The power is turned off. He hovers over me as I work and instructs me in great detail on how the job should be done.

"Why don't you just do it yourself?" I grunt from underneath his workbench, where I am looping the wire into a new outlet.

"I don't do electrical work," he says.

At my house we have worked out an informal division of labor. Once we finish gutting the kitchen together, he goes to work on the carpentry and I start the electrical. Tully's main job is to build a soffit—a false ceiling—which will drop eight inches from the real ceiling around the perimeter of the room. The soffit will allow us to place the cabinets so that there is no gap on top—the sort of space whose only function would be to display a collection of Fiestaware pitchers, which I don't have anyway. ("All it is is a big dust collector," Tully warned.) A soffit will also give me a place to tuck recessed spotlights to illuminate the countertop.

Before Tully can start the carpentry, we again have to use the water level to set an accurate baseline halfway up the wall. We will make all our measurements from this line, which should insure that the cabinets are hung level. We can't use the floor as a guide because it pitches precipitously toward the low point of my sinking support beam in the basement. By now, Tully also has come to accept that I can make an accurate mark on the wall, although he tends to check all measurements three or four times anyway. Sometimes, if he doesn't, he gets into trouble. Several times in recent days he has cut boards the wrong length, walked back from the saw and learned of his mistake, and tried to invent new curses. ("Oh, you louse of all louses!" was one of my favorites.)

"He's getting forgetful," my mother tells me regularly, always when Tully is out of earshot.

It feels good today to be working by myself, although my wrist hurts like hell from a recurring accident I've had with the power drill. I've bored more than a dozen holes into the floor joists using an inch-thick drill bit, and several times the long bit has stuck in the wood, and, before I can react, has started the grip of the drill spinning wildly, twisting my hand along with it.

"Watch that drill," my father says, needlessly, when he happens to be in the basement during one accident. Lately, his harping hardly bothers me. It's his way of showing concern. And he can't act superior in this case. I've seen him twist his wrist in the same way doing this same job with the same drill.

When I finish with the kitchen, I will have replaced every foot of the original wiring in this house, except for two short lengths of switch wires that were buried in the only two walls we left intact. Since I have decided to upgrade to a heavier gauge wire, the stuff I'm pulling through the drilled basement joists gives back a lot of resistance. It is going to be a day-long tug of war.

Bob the Plumber is here today to rough in the plumbing for the new kitchen sink and dishwasher. Since they will be side by side and use the same drainpipe and the same supply lines, it's a quick job for him. "Nothin' to it," he said early this morning. Still, I know he will manage to stretch an hour's job into at least three hours of work—and talk and coffee and cigarettes.

Even though he's charging me by the hour, I don't really care. Bob has become a welcome addition to the crew. I think my father and I both look forward to his arrival to loosen things up. Bob enjoys teasing both of us. When he had finished the upstairs bathroom he looked around and exclaimed, "Now you'll have a nice place to bring all your concubines."

"Oh, yeah, Bob," I told him, "since I moved to Narrowsburg, it's been hot and cold runnin' concubines."

"So, John," he says to me, "now that you're almost done with this place, I suppose you're gettin' ready to sell it and start on another project—a nice big Victorian or somethin'."

"Yeah," I say, "I've been looking around."

Tully grunts. "I hope he was payin' attention," he tells Bob. "If he does another one, I'm not gonna be around to help."

"Oh, c'mon, John," Bob says to my father. "What else would you do with yourself?" The rhetorical nature of the question makes it a punchline—funny and poignant at the same time. Tully misses a beat, as if he's really thinking about it.

"Plenty," he says finally. We know he's dreaming, and he probably knows it, too.

Today Bob works with his usual mix of competence and distraction. A pile of cigarette butts grows in his used Styrofoam coffee cup, and misplaced tools litter the floor around him. But he seems somehow out of sorts. We haven't needed him for anything in months, and he has been slow returning my calls for this job. In between trips to the basement, I try to catch up on the progress of his college classes.

"I'm not in school this semester," he says. "It's been kind of funny this year for me. The wife left me and went off with another guy."

"No kiddin'," Tully says.

"Yeah," Bob says. "She took the young one with her. Everybody else is still livin' with me." Bob may have lost his wife and son, but he is left with two kids at home—*and* his father-in-law and his wife's nephew. "I got five people to feed still," he says.

After Bob finishes his work and drives off, we can talk of nothing else. "How do you like that," Tully says. "She leaves him, and he's stuck with her relatives. That guy has a good heart." Other folks who have renovated houses might tell you there is no such thing, but somehow we have found a plumber with a good heart.

I have been living in a construction zone for many months by now, but the work on the kitchen is the worst disruption. The stove still sits in the middle of the bare room, tethered to the propane supply line, usually covered with a dusty old bedspread and the detritus of whatever work we're doing. One day I see my cat sleeping between the jets with his paw resting on a crowbar and his head on a tape measure. The refrigerator is a big brown hulk in the dining room. The sink and a piece of countertop are sitting in the basement, supported by a homemade frame of two-by-fours and hooked up to the water supply with garden hoses. This means my coffee machine is two flights away each morning, and cooking has become a huge hassle. For lunch we have sandwiches and hope the weather is good enough for us to sit outside on the deck.

Routines develop easily around Tully. I have been putting sandwiches in front of him for months now (though he does all his own cooking at home, he will not lift a hand to feed himself in my house), and every time he looks at his plate and says, "Why so big?" Then he eats the whole thing, along with as many potato chips as I give him. Then he asks where the cookies are. When Uncle Santino is working, he and Tully sit across from each other at the table and talk about the supermarket where they both buy groceries. They can go on for quite a while about "buy one, get one free" specials and triple-coupon policies.

For the first time since we started working, we're actually following plans. Until now, we've made design decisions on the fly, my father often forcing me to reinvent the house—where a doorway will be, where a window will go—at the moment of construction while he stands impatiently with a hammer in his hand.

"C'mon," he says. "Decide, so I can get workin'."

So far this hasn't been a big problem, because most of the choices are simple and obvious. The higher ceilings in the upstairs bedrooms were the most elaborate change, and God knows I am enjoying those ceilings as much as a man can. My only regret is a deep, useless shelf behind the toilet in the upstairs bathroom, which Tully started building before I had a chance to think it through. But I can live with it. And I know better than to complain. Whenever I take my time deciding on something, whether it is the placement of a window or the purchase of a fixture, my father spits out some tobacco juice and observes with a pronounced weariness, "You're worse than a woman." I don't think he would get an argument from any of my women friends.

I have decided to brave his scorn with the kitchen. From the earliest days of this project, I have envisioned it as the hub of the house. I have visions of summer weekends with guests up from the city and great bouts of communal cooking, like scenes from *The Big Chill*, except with Sinatra as the soundtrack. I have even been known to cook for myself, though my skills are rudimentary, my goals never grandiose. I just want the room to be well planned and efficient.

A few weeks ago, I made a trip to Home Away from Home Depot and sat for most of an afternoon with a young woman and a computer, and we designed my dream kitchen. As usual, the range of my dreams is limited by the plain confines of the house. My vision had to fit into a ten-by-twelve box whose sides already contain an exit door which can't be moved, a fixed chimney, and a passage to the dining room, which we have enlarged as much as possible while maintaining enough studs to keep the walls standing. So my imagination is limited to the fairly standard horseshoe-shaped plan. I decide on the classic and labor-efficient layout called the work triangle, with sink, stove, and refrigerator occupying each of the three points. I happily lose a few cabinets to add a new window. Otherwise, most of the creative decisions involve choices between the quality and design of cabinets, and whether they will contain pricey additions like rolling shelves and lazy Susans. I come away with a stack of fairly detailed renderings produced by a computer program. Tully and I have to fill in some blanks, but there should be no surprises.

After some fleeting fantasies of splurging on this room, I've landed back on solid ground. I'm going to buy midrange appliances and low-priced cabinets, just a step above the kind you assemble yourself. I thought of looking for a commercial stove, but to spend a lot of money now for something like a Viking range would seem ridiculous—a bit like installing sonar on a rowboat. I'm going to put commercial-grade vinyl tile on the floor. A single-bowl stainless steel sink seems fine, and I can pick it up for less than a hundred dollars.

I have a good friend who lives on Philadelphia's Main Line who has expanded the kitchen of his modest stone house while I've been working on my renovation. That one room cost more than I'm spending on the entire project. I've read about six-figure price tags for kitchen renovations, and the first thought I have is one my father might be proud of: *You gotta be kiddin' me!* The one concession I'm making to extravagance is a granite countertop. It's an easy extravagance, since the granite comes for free.

Years ago, when he was still working for the city government, Tully watched over the rehabilitation of a building that had once housed the Scranton Dry Goods Company. It was the first serious casualty in the collapse of the city's downtown. During the building's renovation into offices, the workers were tearing out the original granite entrance lobby. Somebody offered my father some pieces, and he took about a dozen rectangular slabs of black-and-white-flecked stone. They had been sitting in his backyard for more than a decade. He'd used a few pieces under one of his concrete birdbaths. Soon after I'd started searching for a house— before we had any idea what kind of kitchen we'd be working with—Tully asked me if I wanted the granite for my kitchen counter. Without a moment's hesitation, I said yes.

He cleaned and stacked the pieces, measured them and marked the dimensions on each one in a careful black script. The stone has been waiting in neat rows near his back fence, next to the old Astrodome dog kennel. Putting that counter in was something I'd been looking forward to. In a house that otherwise had become a little too much like its owner—neat and nice, but somewhat bland—it would be a strong statement of character.

Tully came with me to the Home Depot for the kitchen design session. He looked at the computer screen for a time while the saleswoman and I moved virtual cabinets around. Then he took a short nap in his chair while we worked out the details.

He roused himself and came with us to a sales-floor display when the saleswoman wanted to show me a sample of the cabinets I was considering.

"What kind of countertop are you planning to go with?" she asked.

"We're doing our own with salvaged granite," I told her smugly.

"Oh, that'll be nice," she said.

The sample kitchen we stood in had a lush green granite counter with a beautiful bullnose on the front. The granite was so highly polished and perfect that it didn't look anything like the random pieces sitting in Tully's backyard. It didn't even look like something that had come out of the ground.

Tully went to the counter and started pawing it. "That's not granite," he told the clerk.

"Yes it is," she said.

"Nah, that's not granite." He wrapped his hand around the bullnose and squeezed.

"Yes it is!" she said. "I was here when they installed it. I watched them do it."

"I don't think so," Tully said.

"It is!"

This could have gone on all afternoon. "I don't think we need to argue about this right now," I told them. They looked at me like two school kids who'd been disciplined. We headed back to the computer station.

"That ain't granite," my father whispered to me, loud enough for the woman to hear.

I got my computer drawings and got us out as quickly as I could.

We drove back to Tully's house and sat under his black walnut tree. Now all he wanted to talk about was the countertop. I think he was finally resigned to the fact that he had indeed seen granite and its shiny green perfection disturbed him. There was no way we could match it with the salvaged, irregular pieces.

"How are we gonna put a trim on the front?" he asked me. "We can't get a bullnose like that."

"I don't need a bullnose," I told him. "I've seen granite strips. We could glue them on the front. Or we could use wood for the trim."

"How you gonna attach it?"

"I just said—*glue.*"

Tully shook his head. "I don't know," he said.

"It was your idea to use the granite in the first place," I reminded him. "We'll figure it out."

"I don't know," he said.

After that conversation, I make a drawing of my plan for the counters. We will put down a layer of plywood on top of the base cabinets—two pieces of three-quarter-inch board that will provide lots of support for the stone—and then glue the granite on top. A friend I've made at the Inn while watching the Yankees makes his living producing objects out of slate. He has offered to cut the pieces of granite for us to a uniform size on his heavy-duty wet saw.

When I show my drawing to Tully, he is still pessimistic. Because we are using many pieces of stone—none are more than two feet long—there will be a number of seams. He wonders how we will seal those. Somehow, that seamless expanse of green granite in the Home Depot has intimidated Tully. He can't see past its bright perfection.

"I think you should get somebody to make you a counter-top out of Formica," he says finally, after we argue about the feasibility of our using granite throughout a morning of work. I should admit right then that I am beaten, but I continue to hold out hope for the granite.

Meanwhile, work progresses. I've run new circuits for the refrigerator and lights, and set up a relay of plugs arrayed on the three walls above where the backsplash will go, whatever countertop conclusion we come to. After years of living in apartments where I've sometimes had to run extension cords to the coffee maker, I am installing enough plugs here for some kind of test kitchen. With six double outlets for twelve feet of counter, I could buy a carload of gadgets and run them all at once.

The pots that will hold the spotlights are installed in the soffit. As has become typical in this house, the skeleton of exposed wood is a mélange of old and new, the sand-colored cleanness of new pine mixing with the bourbon brown of boards we've ripped from some other wall. Here and there is a glossy strip of varnished knotty pine saved from the upstairs bedroom. I begin to wonder what the next renovators will say when they tear things apart decades from now. *Who were the cheap bastards who did this job?*

The more we tear apart, the more my father sours on the work of the original builder, Floyd Campfield. Granted, he'd used good materials, but not always in the best way. Tully began to develop a theory early on, when he saw the wavy unevenness of the concrete of the basement floor. He expanded his theory when we discovered that the stairway to my second floor was a few inches off center and that the two-by-fours in one wall had been put in sideways. Tully's theory solidified as we tore away the old Sheetrock on the first floor and discovered that studs were out of line and off center, sometimes defying the simple principle of the plumb bob.

"Jesus," he would say, "they musta been drunk when they did this. Floyd musta had a beer party for these guys." My father doesn't usually drink at a party; to drink at work is beyond his comprehension.

"Well," I'd say, "at least they had fun."

"Yeah, some fun. This place looks like a funhouse."

Luckily, we were going to cover all of Floyd's fun with a half inch of gypsum board. It was time to start Sheetrocking again.

Since those dark days of winter, we have finished a few other rooms, and the process has become almost routine. We start the day like two surgeons prepping for a run-of-the-mill operation, collecting our tools. Tully carries from the basement what he will need: a large T-square, a chalk box, a utility knife and sandpaper to keep the blade sharp. I strap on my tool belt, which by now is worn in, its pocket edges rolled and frayed and a few stains scattered around. I fill the pockets with inch-and-a-quarter screws, put a new blade in my knife, sharpen my pencil, and stick the screw gun into my belt's hammer loop like a weapon. The weather is warm again, and I am wearing those same green cotton pants that I put on for the first day of work. They are fraying and spattered with paint. I have washed my own blood off them more than once. The pants and I both are broken in.

Starting to work, I still have some qualms about doing this job with Tully. I don't want it to turn into another battle of pride and confidence. But it becomes clear during the first hour that our routine has rounded the edges where we bump up against each other. I pull out my measuring tape and check the length we need for a four-foot-wide sheet on the wall. With the soffit dropped from the original ceiling, none of the wall space will require a full eight-foot-high sheet.

Tully positions himself in the dining room, near the heavy stack of pristine boards.

I enter the kitchen and pull out my tape measure.

"Seven, two," I call in.

"Seven, two," Tully repeats.

"Seven, two," I say again.

"Seven, two," he says.

He marks the board on the top edge, flips the T-square into place, and pencils a straight line across the sheet. Then he makes his first slice down the pencil line with the utility knife. With that shallow cut as a guide, he goes back and cuts across the board again. This time, the blade digs deeper. He pushes the cut board away from the pile, leans his body behind it, and snaps the cutoff piece on the line. The paper backing holds it like a hinge, and it swings. Then Tully cuts the paper from behind, and the cut piece falls into his hand. Naturally, he saves every cutoff piece for future use.

Sometimes we reverse roles—him measuring, me cutting—without saying anything to signal the change.

If Tully is cutting, I measure the distance between the wall studs, which is where the screws will bury themselves to hold the Sheetrock in place. In theory, the centers of all the studs should be sixteen inches apart. But either Floyd's crew was not always so careful or the decades of fluctuating temperature and humidity have warped the boards. Near the floor, the studs might be where they belong, but at the ceiling, they are often an inch or more out of place. I know from experience that there is nothing more frustrating when you're wrestling a board into place than driving a screw into nothing but air. So I call in to Tully two measurements for each stud, bottom and top.

"Fifteen," I say.

"Fifteen," he says. "Next?"

"Fifteen and . . . ah, three quarters on top."

"Fifteen and three quarters on top. Okay."

We go on like this through the dozens of studs. There is a rhythm and flow to the work. Richard Russo described a father and son Sheetrocking together in his comic novel *Nobody's Fool.* The tempo of the work is what he noted. "Maybe sheetrocking wasn't one of Sully's favorite jobs," Russo wrote about his fictional father, "but like most physical labor there was a rhythm to it that you could find if you cared to, and that rhythm could get you through a morning."

After I make the stud measurements, I walk into the dining room and wait for Tully to hand me the end of the chalk line. I stretch it down to the mark at the bottom of the board.

"Ready?" he asks.

"Go ahead."

He reaches as far as he can toward the middle of the chalk line and plucks the string with two fingers, lifts it a few inches off the board, and lets it snap back with a soft pop of sound and a puff of blue powder. When the first line is marked, we move without talking to a different set of marks and snap the string again. I remember his yelling at me, "Who taught you how to strike a line?" If he were to ask me now, I could say, "You did."

When the Sheetrock is moved into place, I follow these dusty blue lines to screw it securely to the studs. As we work around the window openings, the number of blue lines increases, forming squares and rectangles across the dull gray surface of the paper. From a distance, the pattern looks like a map of city streets.

Doing this work, often without a word between us that is not a number, I think of those first days of renovation, when I admired the routine efficiency and competence of Lou Meckle and his son. Now, in our own fashion, Tully and I are working the same way. Without remarking on it—almost without realizing it, really—my father and I have become a team. There is a quiet camaraderie to it, a comfort in the pyramid of simple skills whose pinnacle comes to nothing more, or less, than a fresh wall that covers a jumble of wood studs, insulation, and wiring. Sometimes I think this is better than any heart-to-heart talk we could ever have. Together, we are quietly accomplishing something.

Through the ceiling I can hear the soft rubbing sound of my mother mopping my bedroom. She has made weekly visits to my house part of her routine, too. I have become the dream of every old-fashioned Irish mother—a forty-year-old bachelor son whose shirts she can wash and iron and whose bed she can make. If only I'd go ahead and join the priesthood. Rose has designated herself decorator. She has guided my curtain selection with missionary zeal. And one day after the outside painting was done, without telling me, she hung a wreath of blue silk flowers and ribbons on my front door.

Not long after she did this I was drinking at the Inn with Lurch's younger brother Tom. He was usually very friendly, and I liked his wife, who sometimes worked as a bartender. Tom always drank a bottle of Bud, and on this day we talked about his new job with the Roto-Rooter company. Lurch had been fired, so Tom signed on.

"Your house looks real good," he said.

"Thanks, Tom. Thanks a lot. It's been a lot of work."

"I'll bet." He swallowed some beer. "You're gay, right?"

"Ahhhh, no."

"It wouldn't matter to me if you were," Tom said, and took another gulp of beer. He looked at me again. "You're not, huh?

"No."

"Really?"

"Yeah, really," I said. When I finally noticed Rose's wreath, I understood.

The rhythm of the work carries us through a morning. The walls are finished soon after lunch. The only thing that slows us is the large number of electrical boxes placed in the walls for all of my kitchen plugs. Before each board is screwed completely to the wall, Tully has to come back with his knife and cut out the place where the small rectangular box is placed. He has measured the placement of each box from the floor and marked its location in bold black marker on the subfloor. The cutting around the box must be fairly accurate, because the only thing to cover mistakes is a plastic switch cover plate. Tully approaches this job with the concentration of a gem cutter, and usually there is no more gap around the box than the thickness of a dime.

In the afternoon, we start the ceiling. The measuring grows more complicated, and the procedure is made more difficult by the need to heft the heavy Sheetrock above our heads. We are walking on a short scaffold made of metal milk crates and plywood.

A few of the sheets go up quickly, but then we come to the sunken spotlight pots. Now it's tricky. I man the measuring tape.

"Okay," I call to Tully. "From the window side, the light starts at twenty-four inches. The outside edge is thirty and one quarter." We repeat the measurements back and forth several times. He refuses to make a mistake here.

"Once I cut this, it's cut," he says. "We can't use the sheet again if it's wrong."

A few times he walks into the room and looks at me, just to make sure that I'm looking at the board the same way he is. It's easy to get turned around and measure from the wrong end of a sheet. He goes back and takes the small compass that I've had ever since I drew naïve architectural plans as a kid and scribes two circles on the Sheetrock. He sharpens his knife and cuts the circles from the flat sheet.

"I hope we got this right," Tully says, pocketing his knife and lifting the sheet. We do a simultaneous crabwalk onto the short scaffold, duck our shoulders in synch, and turn the sheet over our heads. The edge of the sheet bumps the end of the soffit, and the bottom hits a corner. We adjust together.

"C'mon, you bastard," Tully says.

The piece fits exactly over the round holes. The two circular lamp pots poke through the Sheetrock with barely an eighth of an inch to spare.

Tully grunts. "Look at that," he says. "Perfect. The first time." He moves his raised hands around the board so that I can free one of my hands for the drill. "Go ahead," he says. "Screw it up." Now I know he says this with no irony intended.

The drill makes quick coughing sounds as I drive the short screws into place. When I have secured the sheet well enough to let Tully off duty, he steps down from the scaffold and looks up to admire the work.

"Rose, Rose," he calls to my mother. "Come on down here and look at this. Ya gotta see this. We got it the first time perfect. We're winners."

16.

Finish Work

My birthday is coming around again, and it seems like a good time for another party. This one will do double duty and serve as a housewarming, too. I invite the same New York media friends who helped me have a drunken sendoff long ago, a knot of people from Philadelphia (who, when I think about it, all work in the media, too) and anyone from around Narrowsburg whom I've talked with for more than three minutes. With a deadline before us, we work like demons to make the place look good.

The kitchen is everything I'd hoped it might become, the centerpiece of the project. After we finish Sheetrocking, we put down a tile floor, Tully spreading sticky mastic with a small-toothed trowel and me working behind him, placing foot-square tiles with careful calculation, following the grid of chalklines we've struck as a guide. The only pain of this project is listening to Tully question again and again and again why I've chosen yellow tiles.

"This room is in the northwest corner," I keep telling him. "It gets the least light. It needs to be brightened." All this is true, except for thirty minutes each day. In summer, just before the sun falls behind a hill in Pennsylvania, it filters through the big pine trees behind my house and fills this room with a luminous glow. I had wanted to add a lot of windows to pull in as much light as possible, but there wasn't much wall space to spare. So I tried for an optical illusion of lightness—white cabinets and a bright yellow floor. Plus, there are enough sunken spotlights in the soffit to start a hydroponic garden.

I love the room, from the buttery floor to the operating-room brightness. Even the Formica countertop.

In the end, my father won that battle. After weeks of arguing about using those granite pieces, one day he'd simply dug in his worn heels.

"We can't do it," he said. "Order a countertop from the lumberyard. I'll pay for it."

I didn't argue any further. This was not really a victory for Tully. He'd been beaten by a job that he couldn't quite get his thoughts around. He was putting much more psychic energy into this renovation than I was.

"I haven't had a good night's sleep in a year," he told Bob the Plumber once. "I'm up nights thinkin' how we're gonna do things here." Who knows how many nights he'd tossed and worried over those slabs of granite? My mother took me aside that afternoon and whispered, "I'll be honest with you, he's heartbroken about those countertops. He was scared, but he won't admit it."

A week later, two young guys from the lumberyard lugged a U-shaped hunk of particleboard and polymers into the kitchen and had it set in place and caulked in less than two hours. Their competence was impressive. The simple, pristine beauty of the finished product softened the sting of regret I had about losing what might have been the most impressive conversation piece of the house.

"They knew what they were doin'," Tully said when they left.

"Every man to his own trade," my mother added wisely, then went to work cleaning every newly installed surface, visible or hidden.

After a few days of unpacking glassware and hooking up appliances, we go back to work, back into the basement, where we had begun.

It is hubris, really, that makes me want to add rooms to this little house. After I make the decision to expand, it becomes easy to understand why houses have become gargantuan these days. Here I am, one man, knocking around in six nicely renovated rooms. I can choose between two full baths with ceramic tile and new fixtures and efficient baseboard radiation and adequate lighting and electrical outlets. But that isn't enough.

So, in the last weeks of summer, we descend each morning to the basement, walking down those stairs that Tully had agonized over months and months ago, down to where Donny Scartelli had argued with Reiger the Realtor over the most fundamental question of all—whether the house would stand up.

Out again comes the water level. I am becoming proficient in the use of this obsolete tool. I imagine Tully and me performing feats of leveling on some kind of historical summer-fair circuit, the carpenters of Chautauqua. In the space that was once the garage, we set up level marks to add a floor. It is no easy task, since Floyd and his drunken crew poured a concrete floor that slopes this way and that, puddles in the middle, and climbs toward the walls. This uneven surface defied the use of a normal water-bubble level.

We start with a baseline about waist high and work down from that, stretching guidelines across the space. The object is to find the highest spot of the uneven floor and use it as the mean measurement so that we can be assured of a level floor. When we finally find that point, we strike another, true baseline just above the wavy concrete. Using that mark, we build a wooden frame around the perimeter. We cut two-by-fours to form a support grid within this frame. Next comes the painstaking task of making up for the unevenness of the floor under these boards—carpenters call them sleepers—by using shims to support them. Tully and I crawl and measure and test and reject shims for days. We are building a new floor that will be almost 250 square feet, two small rooms. In all, scores of shims are required. In some places, the concrete is so far below the level board that we can wedge a two-by-four under it. In other spots, the thin end of a cedar shingle does the trick.

When the sleepers are secured, we lay insulation over a bed of rubber to keep the moisture and cold from coming up from the old concrete. Next, we screw plywood onto the sleepers. The resulting subfloor is level to within an eighth of an inch across a twenty-foot length from the back of the basement to the old garage door. Tully and I look at each other.

"Not bad," he says.

Now it is time to build some walls together.

The morning we start this, I am sicker than a dog. Tully would probably allow a sick dog to drag himself off and sleep. I am not so lucky.

He walks through the door with his usual greeting, "What's up?"

"I feel awful," I tell him.

"C'mon," he says, "get your tool belt. Let's get started." Nowadays, he doesn't even laugh when I put my belt on.

Today, for the first time in all our days of working, my father has decided I will labor as an equal. Well, almost.

"You're gonna do this wall," he tells me.

I sense that he is following some kind of script, that he has planned this session. And I think I know what he is doing in his own gruff and clumsy way. Tully is trying to tell me that I've passed the course, that I am ready to move beyond the apprentice stage. I'm not sure if he really believes that to be a fact, but we are running out of things to do.

My test is to put up a wall of two-by-four studs, sixteen inches on center. It will be the back wall of my new room, running from the corner where the electrical box hangs and across the basement to the stairs. There, the wall turns west and runs along the stairs out toward the back of the house.

The top and bottom plates for this wall are already in place. We put them in to frame the floor. I have to measure for the placement of the studs and manipulate the plumb bob to make sure the top and bottom markings are correct. Then I will actually wield the sixteen-ounce graphite hammer that my friends bought me so long ago and nail the studs into place.

Tully can not keep out of the way as much as I think he has planned to. Maybe he feels sorry for me. The repeated bending and straightening required for this job make me sick. Every now and then I have to stop and stand and breathe deeply.

"What the hell's wrong with you?" Tully asks.

"I don't know. I'm sick."

Twice that morning I hurriedly unbuckle my tool belt, drop it to the floor, and run upstairs to the bathroom.

"You feel better now?" Tully asks when I get back.

"No."

"Let's get this wall done."

And we do. We scrape our pencils sharp, play with the plumb bob, saw the boards, hammer those studs into place, and nail them tight. The room we are framing is going to be my music studio. I think at some point in all the pounding how appropriate this is, how this project has brought me full circle. Music is what first took me away from my father. I remember a Saturday not long before I left Scranton. Tully and I traveled to New York City to buy me a new trumpet. He couldn't understand why pieces of pipe cost so much, and he pressured me to buy a less expensive model.

I pouted on the way home with my new, cheap horn. Tully thought I should be grateful. A few wrong words led to an argument, which I ended when I told him, "You don't know anything." For years I believed that. In some ways, he may have believed it, too. Now I know better.

At the end of the day, we have a wall built. It wasn't necessary to put it up, but it's an important wall—my first solo flight as an aspiring carpenter, and permanent support for that sagging basement beam. "That beam's not goin' anywhere now," my father says, pounding a palm on a new stud.

Columns of afternoon sunlight slant into the basement. Sawdust rises in these columns in swirling profusion as Tully sweeps the floor. I stack the leftover boards, fold my tool belt away, and survey our work. It was a simple job, a few dozen boards nailed into place. But to me it seems as if we have built a cathedral. I don't feel lousy anymore.

After that, one last bit of construction remains before the party: finishing the new back entrance to replace the old garage door. We rip apart the overhead door. It produces a pile of metal glides, a bunch of bolts, and four wood panels. Even to Tully, it's junk. In its place we put up another wall, this one as thick as the concrete foundation. Naturally, we use leftover lumber, the thick, wide planks that had supported us on the scaffold. Into this frame we stick a big double-hung window that I bought for fifty dollars at the lumberyard on one of my first visits there, back in the days before all the workers knew my name and when (I guessed) they cringed when they saw me and the cranky old man coming for another visit. I also bought a new entrance door with a long pane of insulated glass built into it. Together, Tully and I hang the window and door, make them square and plumb.

He wants to plaster the outside of this new wall. He arrives one day with a bundle of wire lath in his trunk. I cringe when I see it, remembering the razor edges that had cut me when I crawled through my attic trying to eradicate those sons-a-bitchin' squirrels.

Here it is, I think, *the time at the end of the project when Tully will teach me what he really knows.* This was the work he had done daily for most of his years in construction. It was his trade, the skill he carried in his bones.

As he starts with the wire lath, I am standing around, waiting for instructions. Then Tully says, "You know, this is a one-man job. I don't need help with this. You go ahead and do something else."

What can I say? "You sure?" I ask.

"Yeah."

I realize then that what we have done on this job is what we have done in life. We have recreated in months what we had created over years. We know each other better now, with the comfortable, mundane knowledge people get from working together every day. We have reforged between us not only the links of blood and emotion that connect all fathers and sons but also those peculiar bonds forged of turf and house paint that I'd read about in John Cheever's fiction. Together, we have made this house.

My father and I have come through dark days, when I hated him simply for being what he was. And I'm fairly certain he has felt the same way about me. But we have kept quiet about it. We have arrived at an understanding; we can each brag about the other behind his back. We are what fathers and sons are supposed to be—two different people, separated by decades and held apart by the same powerful force that draws them together, a kind of reverse magnetism of love.

So what does it matter if for this job he doesn't need me? Maybe he just wants to do it by himself, indulge in a solitary nostalgia for the days when he worked with his hands and put food on the table for his family. Perhaps he knows I will just be in the way. I will slow him down. Is that so different from the fact that when I plan a cocktail and dinner party with my friends, the editors and writers from the big cities, I haven't thought to include Tully? He would only slow us down.

Tully does a good job on that stucco. Mixing the mud by hand in small batches, he scoops it onto the hock and then rhythmically trowels it onto the wire lath as if he is icing a cake. Then he uses a soft trowel to float a smooth finish. The new wall blends nearly perfectly with the original concrete foundation that surrounds it.

He is washing the mud off his tools when I come down to inspect the work.

"It's been a long time since I did that," he says. "It looks pretty good, doesn't it?"

"Not bad," I tell him.

"I'm more or less proud of myself," my father says.

I have my housewarming. The two days when the guests are there go by in a blur. It seems I am constantly giving house tours on which I show my sophisticated friends the higher ceilings in the bedrooms, the refinished and polished floors, the gleaming fixtures, the Martha Stewart paint, the window treatments. My friends are politely and appropriately impressed. Although I have removed the wreath from the front door, a few of them interrupt my tour speech to tease me. "Are you sure you're not gay?" they ask.

My birthday is a perfect late summer Sunday, sunny and breezy and dry and warm. I've hired a jazz trio to play under a tent in the backyard, and I spend much of the time sitting in. Tully sits on the deck through most of the party, explaining the construction process in great detail to anyone who asks. I am fixing something in the kitchen when I hear him say, proudly, "John did all the wiring himself."

Uncle Santino sits quietly on the deck and listens. My mother mingles, doing her best to reveal the most embarrassing information about my youth in the shortest possible time. At one point, I have to put down my trumpet and go to rescue John, the hardware store owner, when I see that Rose has him pinned against a tree.

"I know more about you now than I think I want to," John tells me, escaping toward the house.

Through the afternoon, I keep anticipating the primal roar that will signal Lurch's arrival. He seemed excited when I invited him. But he doesn't show.

When it comes time for my birthday cake, I am a little bit drunk and ready to give a speech. I haven't written anything down, but for a few days I've been composing something in my head.

I can't thank my family enough, I planned to say. *They've been more help to me than I could ever deserve. My mother has made getting me the right curtains and throw rugs her life's* mission. *My uncle has carefully and patiently sanded down and painted over most of my mistakes.*

Then I will direct the crowd's attention to the new wall my father has plastered and tell the story of how he gave himself a small, tentative compliment when it was done.

"I'm more or less proud of myself," he said. *Well, he deserves to be. I'm more or less proud of him, too.*

But when I blow out the candles, Tully is nowhere to be seen, and the crowd seems completely uninterested in speeches. I eat my piece of cake and keep quiet. Keeping quiet is more my family's style anyway. A few hours later, the party is over and everyone has gone home, and I am alone in my new house with a lot of empty bottles. I clean up and close the windows. Fall is a few days off, and the nights are cool. A few times I stop whatever I'm doing and just stand and stare at things we have built. When I left the city, I felt all in pieces. Putting things together out here has somehow renovated me, too. Today I have crossed officially into middle age, and it is time to get on with my life.

Epilogue
Another River

I am writing this near another river, in another place. At present, I am, as Henry David Thoreau informed his readers at the beginning of *Walden*, a sojourner in civilized life again.

Most of what is written here was set down not within sight of the twisting Delaware River but just a stroll away from the slick, pungent shores of the East River. I have come back to Manhattan.

My sojourn in the city this time around is in an apartment on the far eastern edge of the island, where I hold the legal lease (and pay twice as much rent as I did for the old place in the East Village). My landlord is a giant insurance company that built its own high-rise village in the crowded city fifty years ago. But like my old place, my new apartment is noisy as hell sometimes. The teenager in the apartment next door plays rap on her stereo and Beatles tunes clumsily on the piano. It often seems that the folks upstairs are bowling. The trash trucks line up outside my window at seven-thirty in the morning and usually spend an hour or more methodically crushing things. And, oddly, it all sounds like music to me.

I am still a walker in the city. But these days I can't pick up the trail of tears. I tread uptown to see Alfred Brendel play Mozart at Carnegie Hall. Into the theater district to meet a musician friend for dinner when he is between performances of a Broadway show. Downtown for lunch with a writer friend at a perennially trendy place where a major movie star is seated across the room and we sneak glances, pretending not to care. The chance to do all these things on any given day is why people come to New York City. Out of the tumult of what I was feeling in those days that I drove—fled—from the city to find a house, one thought has stayed with me: Why would anyone live anywhere else? When I walk around the city now, I feel like laughing, such is my good fortune.

Gradually, I have begun to insinuate myself back into that weird world I left behind—the swirl of cocktail parties and professional gossip. It's interesting again because I know I can live without it. I skip more parties than I once dared. And I'm not invited to much anyway. Leave the city, and you are easily and quickly forgotten.

Sometimes I'll run into someone I haven't seen in a long time. "Where have *you* been?" he or she will ask.

"I left town for a while," I report, distilling my answer to its essence. "I went out to the country and renovated a house with my father. He's a construction worker. And I'm not."

It seems that everyone to whom I tell this says to me, "Would you and your father want to come and do some work at my place?"

Fat chance. I can answer my mother's question definitively now. No, I don't think I could ever be a construction worker. But a whole new world has opened up to me. Some of Tully's rough-hewn lessons actually sank in. I came to this project not knowing how to hammer a nail, and now I know how to hammer a nail. I have a new understanding that there is a world of aptitude and achievement inherent in that simple act. I've learned, often the hard way, that I can make something other than a pile of paper. Along with the burns and scrapes and bruises and humiliations big and small comes a sense of competence that fills some empty place I had. Maybe in some way I wanted to be more like the old man. Now I am, if only a little.

There is a new woman in my life, and she is sensible and generous and wonderful in ways that I'd never imagined. We met at Narrowsburg's first international film festival, an event which would require a whole other book to explain. She's a Texan who came to New York two decades ago and got into the television business. Jana has taken to Tully in a big way. He built her flower boxes so that in the summertime she could turn the deck of my house into something more attractive than a storeroom for unused lumber.

My father made the boxes back home in Scranton, in Fort Tully, then disassembled them, carefully labeled each piece—A-1, A-2, etc.—and packed them into the trunk of his old gray Toyota, which he has now repaired with strips of pink sheet metal riveted over the rusty fenders. Jana watched while Tully and I reassembled the pieces, turning this relatively simple job into yet another lap in our marathon running argument. After Tully left she said to me, "You are *so* much your father's son." And I pretended to have no idea what she was talking about.

Back in the city, I often find myself over on this other river. I have become fat as a cow, and I plod along the shoreline promenade, jogging to lose my rural girth. When the sun is out, the light on the water can be miraculous. It makes garbage skows sparkle like cruise ships. My waterfront companions are fishermen playing salsa on boom boxes, models on Rollerblades in the private trance of earphones, and vagrants taking the sun on benches. All of it, the sights and sounds and feel of the day, nearly lift me off the pavement. At those times, even in my sweaty, grunting pain, I realize that when Jana tells me, as she often does, "You have a wonderful life," I cannot pretend to have no idea what she is talking about.

There is a point on my jog where the river bends sharply to the west. As I round the turn, the Statue of Liberty appears, small and distant, framed by the huge stone pillars of the Brooklyn Bridge and the proscenium of the hanging roadway. In my fatness, I always want to stop running there, but the sight of the statue makes me keep going. I always think of my father then. Tully might not see the symbolism here that I do. In fact, he'd probably be more interested in the cement plant across the East River that juts into the water like the prow of a ship. I wheeze and run on toward the statue, realizing that I am just one generation removed from that island in the bay and all the confusion and hope and striving to which it bore witness. My father has performed the modern miracle of America. Somehow, he made sure that my life was better than his. Whatever house I inhabit, I realize, is built mostly by him.

Tully may not have raised me in a cultural sense. There are writers and musicians and even a few college professors who played that surrogate role. But he is my father in the ideal sense. He has been there when I needed him. He has given me a great gift, and my one fear is that I may not be like him in ways that are substantial and important, and that when my time comes to return the favor, I won't be up to the task.

I look at the city now in a new way. Some days I'll stop and spend twenty minutes watching workers erect a scaffold. At a cocktail party on a roof deck in Tribeca, I stand in the shadow of the World Trade Towers with my sweaty glass and tell my hosts how a good power washing would do wonders for their deck.

A new sense of competence in my surroundings has spilled over to strange little problems that not long ago would have left me frustrated and a little poorer. In my city apartment, I wire my own lights. I hang shelves. I have even started to refinish furniture, taking a piece I picked up for fifty bucks and, after hours of stripping and sanding and staining and polishing, turning it into something worth almost half that. A tape gets stuck in my VCR, and I take the cover off and get it out. (The nearest repairman wanted sixty dollars just to bring it in the door.) My coffee grinder stops, and I take it apart and get it working again. (I'd already thrown away two machines because—I was to find—a piece of plastic slipped off a little spring.) Screwing the repaired machine back together gives me a feeling of accomplishment that I've never had from my real job.

"The thinking classes are fatally removed from the physical side of life," the late sociologist Christopher Lasch wrote soon before he died. "Their only relation to productive labor is that of consumers. They have no experience of making anything substantial or enduring."

My house will endure. The experience of rebuilding it has helped me endure, and its pull on me is powerful. I never spend more than a month in Manhattan before I am overcome by the urge to visit. Some days the drive is like entering a postcard for two hours. Arriving, I turn on the heat, and while the house warms I drop by the Inn for a drink and chat with Miss Mary, trying to catch up on the local gossip. I'm trying not to spend so much time at the Inn, but I doubt I will ever be a damn soda drinker. Lurch and Anna come in and wave and sit at the other end of the bar. Lurch sucks down a bottle of his beer and walks over my way.

"You hunt?" he asks.

"No."

"I've been watchin' a couple of six-pointers hangin' around that gully behind your house. Is anybody gonna hunt on your land? Could I hunt on your land?"

"Sure," I tell him. "Go ahead."

Lurch gets as happy as a man can be. He shakes my hand. "You made my day," he shouts. He skips into a little dance around the bar. "You made my day."

"What got you so excited?" his wife yells over.

"I'll tell you later," Lurch says, and keeps dancing. When the snow comes, he will plow my driveway without my asking. No, I'll never be a true Woodchuck, but now and then I get honorary status.

I am making a life in this town, gradually working my way into its comfortable corners. I know where to go and jump in the river on hot summer evenings, as the sky changes colors over my head and not another soul is in sight. I've found a place where I can sit on the riverbank and watch eagles fish. I know a country road to run on that in a few short miles takes me past expansive farm fields and tight ravines where water drips softly from mossy rocks. Often, the roadside is a soft bed of pine needles.

I sometimes walk the three miles into town by following the railroad tracks that shadow the river. As I sidle down the slope behind my house, I look for deer. I've seen them pass through my property many times, sneaking single file like a quiet reconnaissance patrol. Usually, they swoop in from the east, from across the road, and stop and eat whatever it is they can find (including my potted flowers), then head for the river. One night I looked out from the kitchen window and saw a young spike buck with his front hooves on my deck, nibbling on a potted plant.

I've also seen a red fox sitting like a sentinel in my backyard. He showed up every night for a week or so. He always seemed to come from the west, the opposite direction from the deer. I was worried he would kill my cat, and I shouted at him and waved my arms and finally threw stones. But he was defiant in his routine. Then he disappeared. A while later I was walking the tracks to town, and I came upon a fox carcass nearly stripped to the bones by the birds. The long bone of a deer leg was still clamped in his jaws. I wondered if this was the same fox and whether I should get myself a gun. I guess I could call Lurch.

In town, some days it takes an hour just to drop by the post office. The director of the local summer opera company comes over to ask if I can help her find musicians for next season. I stop in to say hello to Dave, who used to cook me my lonely dinners at the Inn and now has his own restaurant on Main Street. The editor of the local paper says hello. Once she asked if she could borrow that power washer I'd been bragging about. Too late—Tully took it for himself. I go by the lumberyard for some paint, and they ask me where I've been. Reiger the Realtor spots me, and we chat. He always pitches new fixer-uppers that have come on the market. "I don't think I'm up for that," I tell him.

"What about your father?" he asks.

My father, after some moping, has tried to move on, too. After the party, we worked for a few more weeks, finishing the basement. One of the last jobs was putting down a parquet floor.

"What's wrong with linoleum?" Tully asked several times.

I knew enough by now not argue the issue. I drove to Home Away from Home Depot and bought parquet blocks— the less expensive stuff, of course. Once again, Tully worked the trowel and I set the pieces, moving around the room on our knees like two penitents. When it was finished, it looked good. Uncle Santino was so impressed that he went out and bought me special floor cleaner and a new broom.

Bob the Plumber liked it, too. He made his last return visit to run heat into the basement rooms. He looked awful when he showed up early one morning. His new life as a single man was off to a rocky start. "They took me out to a party last night," he said, "and I had my first drink in seventeen years. And my second. *And* my third . . ."

"You better watch yourself," Tully told him.

"Yeah, I know," Bob said sheepishly. Then, to change the subject, he looked around and yelled, "This place looks great! You get some heat down here and this place'll be nice and snug in the winter."

"I don't think I'll be here much this winter," I said.

"Where ya goin'?" Tully asked.

"Back to New York."

He was quiet for a moment. "Who's gonna take care of the place?"

"The place will take care of itself. Lots of people around here shut down their houses in the winter."

"Well, maybe we'll keep comin' up, once or twice a week."

"Suit yourself," I told him.

I moved back to Manhattan, and the next time I came out to Narrowsburg, the basement was further transformed (though the heat has never quite worked right). Tully just kept working while I was away. He put a closet under those basement stairs that had gone up so slowly so long ago. On the sloped ceiling of the closet were knotty pine panels. He was determined to use every piece we'd torn from the upstairs. Across from the closet, he'd spackled and painted the walls where I'd learned my queasy carpentry. Trim dressed the bottom edges.

Over near the furnace, Tully and Santino had built me a workbench. It was made of two-by-fours and plywood, with a metal sheet screwed down on the work surface. A new red vise commanded one corner. There were plastic containers full of screws and bolts and washers. A clamp light hung from an exposed joist above the bench and was plugged into an outlet ten feet away with an extension cord. I would have run wiring over and installed a new fixture, but Tully still doesn't do electrical work. I may get around to putting up a permanent light someday.

On the sidewall behind the bench, they'd installed a pegboard, and my tools hung on hooks there. Screwdrivers, scrapers, and my tool belt—comfortably creased and greasy. Many of the tools are still officially my father's. I think now that these tools will be his real legacy for me—the tools and the house that those tools helped rebuild. And my newfound ability to pick up one of those tools and have at least a vague idea what to do with it. It turns out that tearing down a wall isn't as easy as I thought. But it's worth the work. Considering where I was when we started working, I believe it has helped to change me back to what I really am. My father and I have something in common after all: this house.

Near the bottom corner of the pegboard hung my expensive graphite hammer, a little the worse for wear, scarred by the many mistakes I'd made, by the tearing down of walls, the stripping of aluminum siding, the building of partitions.

Next to it hung my father's hammer, far more worn than mine, red with its black grip and circle of electrical tape. If there was a symbol for what we had done, there it was, our hammers hanging side by side.

There might come a day when I won't quite recall what led me out to this little house in the first place. But I will remember those two hammers hanging together for the rest of my days.

Acknowledgments

It would be impossible to give enough thanks to the Marchese family for their generosity and support through the entire project. They spoil me, thank God.

A number of people helped with the construction of the house. Bob Hart ran phone lines. Jerry Jacquinot lent tools. Don Scartelli Junior lent expertise, as did Jerry Gans. Lafe Wilmarth brought his artistry with tape and spackle. Jack Lee and Harold K. Jones gave discounts. The folks at Narrowsburg Lumber, especially Bill Grund, were always helpful.

Arlene Lawrence and Richard Socher helped me live in both the city and the country, as did Hilary Sterne. Steve Fishman and Cristina Page shared with me whatever they had that I needed. Ronnie Polaneczky and Noel Weyrich provided me with yet another home away from home. Jana DeHart has filled my life with flowers and jubilance.

A number of people helped with the construction of the book. Marjorie Braman, Charlie Conrad, and Becky Cabaza gave me early encouragement. Mary South gave me a contract. Cindy Spiegel provided direction. Chris Knutsen got his hands dirty and hammered out a manuscript. He's a craftsman.

David Black was there since before the beginning. He's a great agent—nudge, friend, harpie, moneylender, weightlifter, and wine lover.

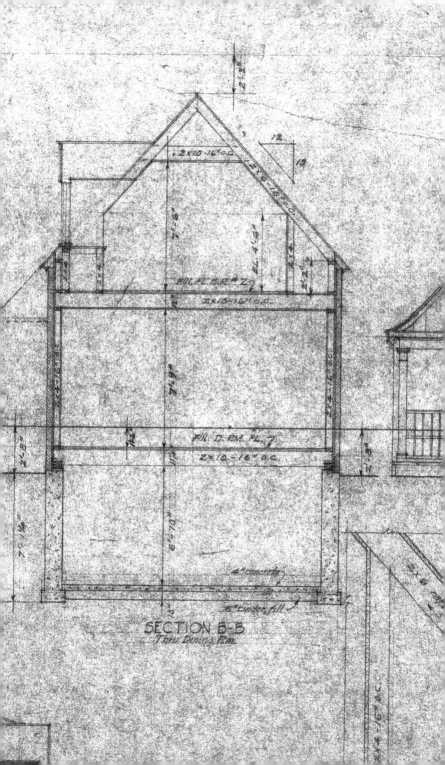

SECTION B-B
Thru Dining Rm.